Structure & Speaking Practice
Moscow

Australia • Brazil • Mexico • Singapore • United Kingdom • United States

NATIONAL GEOGRAPHIC
L E A R N I N G

National Geographic Learning,
a Cengage Company

Structure & Speaking Practice, Moscow

James R. Morgan and Nancy Douglas

Publisher: Sherrise Roehr

Executive Editor: Laura LeDréan

Managing Editor: Jennifer Monaghan

Digital Implementation Manager,
Irene Boixareu

Senior Media Researcher: Leila Hishmeh

Director of Global Marketing: Ian Martin

Regional Sales and National Account
Manager: Andrew O'Shea

Content Project Manager: Ruth Moore

Senior Designer: Lisa Trager

Manufacturing Planner: Mary Beth
Hennebury

Composition: Lumina Datamatics

For permission to use material from this text or product,
submit all requests online at **cengage.com/permissions**
Further permissions questions can be emailed to
permissionrequest@cengage.com

Student Edition: Structure & Speaking Practice, Moscow
ISBN-13: 978-0-357-13796-3

National Geographic Learning
20 Channel Center Street
Boston, MA 02210
USA

Locate your local office at **international.cengage.com/region**

Visit National Geographic Learning online at **ELTNGL.com**
Visit our corporate website at **www.cengage.com**

Printed in China
Print Number: 02   Print Year: 2019

Photo Credits

Unit / Lesson	Video	Vocabulary	Listening

Grammar	Pronunciation	Speaking	Reading	Writing	Communication
Participial and prepositional phrases Review of the present perfect	Stress: Verb + preposition	Interrupting someone politely	**Viral news** Use background knowledge Sequence events Make connections Summarize	Share personal information	Ranking behaviors Catching up at a reunion
The passive voice: simple present and simple past Connecting ideas with *because, so, although / even though*	Stress on nouns and verbs with the same spelling	Asking about companies / Emphasizing important points	**Life without ads?** Identify a point of view Draw conclusions Scan for details	Write a product review	Presenting facts about your city or region Creating a commercial
Embedded questions The passive with various tenses	Negative questions to confirm information	Offering another opinion	**When the seas rise** Use background knowledge Make predictions Take notes on key details Infer meaning Summarize Give opinions	Give an opinion on new construction	Taking a quiz about the world Choosing a civic project
Too and *enough* Future real conditionals	Using pauses in public speaking	Language for presentations	**People of all ages** Use background knowledge Make predictions Infer information Infer meaning Read for details Draw conclusions	State your opinion about a future event	Completing and talking about a lifestyle survey Giving a speech about a solution to a problem

Language Summaries p. 66   Grammar Notes p. 69

1 GETTING INFORMATION

Look at the photo. Answer the questions.

1 Where are these people?

2 What do you think they're talking about?

3 What do you talk about most often with your friends?

UNIT GOALS

1 Identify who someone is and where something is

2 Interrupt someone politely

3 Talk about how you get news and information

4 Share recent news about yourself and others

People talk at a cafe in Montevideo, Uruguay.

Pocahontas County, West Virginia

1 **VIDEO** A Unique US Town

A The video is about a town in a *quiet zone*. What do you think a quiet zone is?

B ▶ What do people say about life in Green Bank, West Virginia? Watch the video and complete the sentences.

1. "Just listen to _____ all around you."

2. "No one here has a _____."

3. "There's a long list of _____ conveniences that we can't utilize here."

4. "We can't _____ because I don't have service."

5. "I really enjoy it because it's _____, it's peaceful, it's _____."

C 🔁 Would you want to live in a quiet zone? Why or why not? Tell a partner.

2 VOCABULARY

When we were younger, my brother and I **argued** a lot...

...but now we **share** everything. We have great **conversations**.

Word Bank				
Verbs				**Nouns**
argue converse chat gossip talk[1]	<u>with</u> someone <u>about</u> something	get into an ~ strike up / start a ~, carry on a ~ have[2] a ~, stop by for a ~ a ~ of (the plan) give a ~, listen to a ~		argument conversation chat discussion talk
discuss share	something <u>with</u> someone	the latest ~, juicy ~, a piece of ~		gossip

[1]You can also *talk <u>to</u> someone*.

[2]*Have* can also be used before *argument*, *conversation*, *discussion*, and *talk*.

A 🔁 Look at the verbs in the Word Bank. All of them are related to talking. Answer the questions with a partner.

> What does "argue" mean?
>
> It means to fight or disagree with someone when you are talking.

1. How are the verbs similar? How are they different? Ask your partner. Use your dictionary to help you if necessary.

2. Which verbs have a negative meaning? Circle them.

3. Which verbs have an identical noun form? Underline them.

B 🔁 Ask and answer the questions with a partner.

1. When is the last time you **got into an argument** with someone? Who was it with? What was it about?

2. Are you good at **striking up conversations** with people you don't know well? Why or why not?

3. How often do you **chat** with your neighbors?

4. Think of a well-known celebrity. What is **one piece of** juicy **gossip** about him or her?

5. What is one thing you want to **discuss** with your instructor?

6. Who do you **share** your personal thoughts with? Why do you choose that person?

7. Who do you **talk to** on a daily basis? What do you **talk about**?

> I got into an argument with my mom yesterday. She's always telling me to clean my room!

3 LISTENING

A Look at the names of the websites below with a partner. Add one more. Which one(s) do you know? Which one(s) do you use?

Facebook	Qzone	Twitter
Instagram	LinkedIn	Mixi
Sina Weibo		

our idea: _____

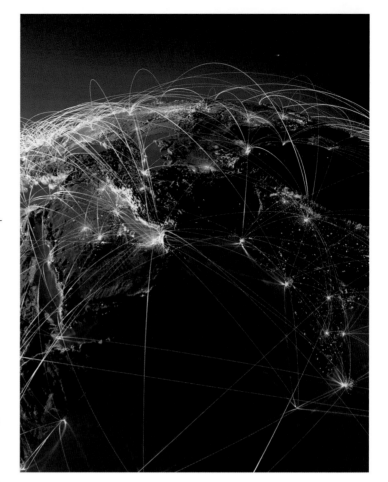

B 🔊 **Infer information.** Read the questions. Then listen to an advertisement for a new online service. Which question might you ask with the service? **Track 1**

a. Do you own a phone?

b. Can I borrow your phone?

c. What's an affordable phone?

d. What's the best thing about phones?

C 🔊 **Listen for details.** Listen again. Complete the summary about InstaHelp and how it works. **Track 1**

When you have a question, it's easy to waste time looking for (1.) _____ online.

InstaHelp is an (2.) _____ service. You ask an important (3.) _____ by

(4.) _____ or instant message. InstaHelp (5.) _____ it on to some of your online

(6.) _____ (and their acquaintances, too). You then get live answers back in

(7.) _____ minutes or so.

D Look back at your answers in **C** and explain to a partner how the InstaHelp service works. Would you use it? Why or why not?

E 🔊 **Pronunciation: Stress: Verb + preposition.** Look at the two underlined words in each question. Which one is stressed? Circle it. Listen and check your answers. **Track 2**

1. Who do you <u>talk</u> <u>to</u> when you have a problem?

2. What do you <u>talk</u> <u>about</u> with your friends?

3. What is everyone <u>gossiping</u> <u>about</u> these days?

4. Do you need to <u>discuss</u> anything <u>with</u> your teacher?

5. Who do you <u>chat</u> <u>with</u> the most on the phone?

F Practice saying the questions in **E**. Ask and answer the questions with a partner.

4 SPEAKING

A 🔊 Listen to and read the conversation. Answer the questions. **Track 3**

1. What does Jared need?

2. What is Ana's advice?

3. Does Jared know Ms. Ruiz? How do you know?

ANA: Oh, look... there's Gloria Ruiz. Do you know her?

JARED: No, I don't. Who is she?

ANA: She's the VP of Marketing for Global Industries. She's standing right over there.

JARED: Is she the tall woman in the sweater?

ANA: No, Gloria is the woman with glasses. She's chatting with the man in the suit.

JARED: You know, I *am* looking for a job.

ANA: You should talk to her. Maybe she can help you.

JARED: That's a good idea. Thanks!

....

JARED: Excuse me, Ms. Ruiz? May I interrupt for a moment? My name is Jared Levy....

B 🔄 Practice the conversation with a partner.

SPEAKING STRATEGY

C 🔄 Think of a time you interrupted someone. Who were you talking to? What were you talking about? Tell a partner.

> My friend and I were having a discussion about our homework. I interrupted because my bus was coming!

D 👥 Role-play. Work in groups of three. Use the Useful Expressions to help you.

Student 1: You are at a party. You need to interrupt two people who are having a conversation. Choose a reason below.

- You think you know Student 2. You want to introduce yourself.

- You need directions from the party to another place.

- Your idea: _____

_____

_____

Useful Expressions: Interrupting someone politely
Introducing yourself
Excuse me. May I interrupt for a moment? My name is...
I'm sorry to interrupt. / I beg your pardon.
I just wanted to introduce myself. My name is...
Interrupting someone you know
Excuse me. Sorry to bother you, (name), but I have a question.
Could I interrupt for a second? I just wanted to say / ask something.

Students 2 and 3: You are chatting. Student 1 will interrupt your conversation. Ask him or her at least two questions.

5 GRAMMAR

A Turn to pages 69–70. Complete the exercises. Then do **B–D** below.

Participial and Prepositional Phrases		
Who is Joe Ortega?	He's the guy	chatting on the phone. on the phone.
Who is Ms. Anh?	She's the woman	wearing glasses. in front of the class.
Which books are mine?	They're the ones	lying on the floor. in the drawer.

Prepositions

against the wall
alongside the house
between the desks
by the road
in the suit
on the table
opposite the door
under(neath) the tree
with the glasses

B Match the questions with their answers. Then use the words in the box to complete the answers with the correct prepositions and verb forms.

argue	between	discuss	hide	~~in~~	in
in	on	~~play~~	with	with	under

1. Who's the leader of the band?
2. Which one is your sister?
3. Which one is my package?
4. Which one is your cat?
5. Who are your friends?
6. Who's Tom?

a. He's the student _____ his grade _____ the instructor.

b. He's the guy __in__ the hat _playing_ the guitar.

c. They're the people _____ the cafe _____ about politics.

d. She's the girl _____ the ponytail _____ the skateboard.

e. It's the one _____ _____ the bed.

f. It's the one _____ the hall _____ the two tables.

C 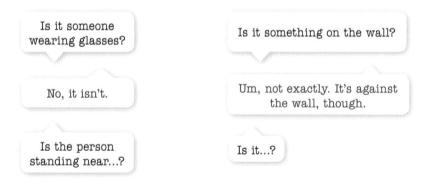 Work with a partner. Follow the steps to play a guessing game.

1. Think of an object and a person that you can see in your classroom. Don't tell your partner!

2. Ask *Yes / No* questions to identify your partner's object and person.

> Is it someone wearing glasses?

> No, it isn't.

> Is the person standing near...?

> Is it something on the wall?

> Um, not exactly. It's against the wall, though.

> Is it...?

D Switch roles and play the game again.

6 COMMUNICATION

A 👥 What do the quotes mean? Discuss with a small group. Share your ideas with the class.

"Great minds discuss ideas. Average minds discuss events. Small minds discuss people."
—Eleanor Roosevelt

"Never argue with stupid people. They will drag you down to their level and then beat you with experience." —Mark Twain

"Silence is one of the great arts of conversation." —Chinese proverb

B 🔁 Think about the ways you communicate. Do you agree with any of these quotes? Explain your opinions to a partner.

C Read the situations below. Which behaviors bother you the most? Put them in order from 1 (most annoying) to 5 (least annoying).

A person / People…

_____ talking loudly on the phone on the train.

_____ having an argument in a restaurant.

_____ gossiping loudly about someone else.

_____ chatting during a movie.

_____ discussing sensitive political issues during dinner.

> Which situation is most annoying to you?
>
> It's definitely when a person talks loudly on the phone on the train. That behavior really bothers me!

D 👥 Form a small group. Tell your group members your answers for the most and least annoying behaviors in **C**. Explain your answers.

1 VOCABULARY

A Look at the words below in blue. Are there any you don't know? Work with a partner to learn their meanings. Then take the quiz on your own.

1. How do you typically **get your news**? ☐ TV   ☐ radio   ☐ online   ☐ other

2. I am most interested in... because _____.
   ☐ **international** (world) **news**   ☐ **local news** (about my town or city)
   ☐ **national news** (about my country)

3. What's one popular **news program** or **news site** in your country? _____
   What kind of news show or site is it?

   entertainment / **international** / **local** / **national** / **sports** / **tabloid** news

   Do you ever watch this news program or visit the site? _____

4. When you read an interesting news **story**, do you post it online? _____

5. Think of someone famous who was **in the news** recently. Who was it? _____
   Was the news about this person **bad**, **good**, **great**, **sad**, or **sensational**? _____
   Did the news about the person **spread** from place to place quickly? _____

6. Think again about the **news story** in #5. How did you **hear the news**?
   ☐ on TV   ☐ on the radio   ☐ on social media   ☐ online
   ☐ by **word of mouth** (= someone told me)
   Did you **tell anyone** else **the news**? If so, how many people did you tell? _____

B Explain your quiz answers to a partner.

> How do you typically get your news?

> Usually online, I guess. I never watch TV.

2 LISTENING

A  **Make predictions.** You will hear two reporters talk about three stories that were in the news recently. Which one (a, b, or c) do you think most people wanted to read or hear about? Circle your answer and then tell a partner.

a. news about jobs and the economy

b. the president's meeting in Asia

c. a scandal involving a soccer player

B 🔊 **Check predictions.** Listen and check your answer in **A**. Track 4

C 🔊 **Listen for details; Infer information.** Read the sentences. Then listen to the full conversation and circle *True* or *False*. Correct the false sentences. Track 5

1. The woman feels that a lot of news today is too sensational.	True	False
2. The man says news today is trying to educate the public.	True	False
3. The man says the least popular news stories are about murder and sports.	True	False
4. The woman believes there should be more news about the economy and the environment.	True	False

D  Discuss the questions with a partner.

1. Do you agree with the opinions in **C**? Why?

2. Think of a story that was in the news a lot recently. Do you think it was important? Why or why not? How long was it in the news?

3 READING 🔊 Track 6

A  **Use background knowledge.** Look at the title. What is a viral news story? Can you think of one example? Tell a partner.

B **Sequence events.** Read the first news story. Number the events in the order they happened. Then retell the story to a partner using the appropriate verb forms.

a. _____ Lulu barks like a dog.

b. _____ Lulu is adopted.

c. _____ Ken is unconscious.

d. _____ The family finds Ken.

e. _____ Lulu goes everywhere with Ken.

f. _____ Lulu's mother dies.

g. _____ Ken has an accident.

C **Make connections.** Read the second news story. What do these pairs of items have in common? Write your answers and then compare them with a partner's.

1. visit waterfalls / go horseback riding
   These are things you can do in Vanuatu.

2. scuba diving / snorkeling _____
   _____

3. three meters below the surface / near Port Vila _____
   _____

4. buy waterproof postcards / receive a special stamp _____
   _____

D **Summarize.** Why do you think each news story went viral? Give a reason for each story. Discuss with a partner.

VIRAL NEWS

A *viral news* story spreads quickly, usually online, and becomes very popular.

Lulu to the Rescue!

Lulu is a kangaroo. For ten years she has lived with the Richards family. Lulu was adopted by the family after they found her next to her dead mother, not far from the Richards family's home in New South Wales, Australia.

Ken Richards is a farmer. He was working on his farm when a heavy tree branch suddenly fell on top of him and he passed out.[1]

Lulu stood next to Mr. Richards's body. She started barking and didn't leave Mr. Richards's side.

"I've never heard Lulu bark like that—she sounded like a dog. She barked and barked, and she didn't stop," said Celeste, Mr. Richards's daughter.

After 15 minutes, the Richards family went to investigate.[2] They found Ken on the ground.

"Lulu is a hero," said Celeste. "She saved my father."

Craig Middleton, a veterinarian, says that Lulu's story is rare. "I have never seen a kangaroo act like that. Maybe Lulu helped Ken Richards because the Richards family is the only family she has ever known."

Lulu is a loyal, friendly, and very intelligent kangaroo. After Ken leaves the hospital, he is planning to go everywhere with Lulu.

This Post Office is All Wet

The Republic of Vanuatu has recently been in the news—but not for the usual reasons.

Approximately 175,000 people live in the Republic of Vanuatu, an island chain east of Australia. It is a popular tourist destination because there's a lot to do there: you can visit waterfalls, go horseback riding, or visit a traditional Ni-Vanuatu village. Vanuatu is most famous for its scuba diving and snorkeling.

In an effort to draw attention to these popular water sports, Vanuatu has created a world's "first": the government has opened an underwater post office. You have to be a trained scuba diver to work there. The office is three meters below the surface in an area outside Port Vila, the capital city.

So far, the post office has hired four workers. They will work in a room surrounded by the beauty of Vanuatu's underwater world. Customers will buy waterproof postcards on land and then dive down to the post office to receive a special waterproof stamp!

[1] If you *pass out*, you fall down and lose consciousness.
[2] If you *investigate* something, you look at it carefully.

4 GRAMMAR See pages 80–82 for more practice with the present perfect tense.

A Turn to pages 70–71. Complete the exercise. Then do **B–D** below.

Review of the Present Perfect					
Question word	*have / has*	Subject	Past participle		Answers
	Have	you	heard	the news?	Yes, I **have**. I heard it this morning.* No, I **haven't**. What happened?
How long	**have**	you	been	a reporter?	(I**'ve been** a reporter) **for** six months.
	has	she			(She**'s been** a reporter) **since** May.

*When you answer a present perfect question with a specific time expression, use <u>the simple past</u>:
Have you heard the news? Yes, I <u>heard</u> it <u>this morning</u>.

B Unscramble the questions.

1. read / you / any funny / have / recently / news stories

   _____

2. in English / ever / have / you / watched / the news

   _____

3. studied / how long / you / English / have

   _____

4. studied / another / have / language / ever / you

   _____

5. known / your best friend / have / you / how long

   _____

C 🔁 Ask and answer the questions in **B** with a partner. Write your partner's answers below. Then ask a follow-up question.

Example: _Yoshi has known his best friend for ten years. They met in elementary school._

1. _____
2. _____
3. _____
4. _____
5. _____

> So you've known your best friend for ten years. Where did you meet?

> In elementary school.

D 👥 Tell another pair one thing you learned about your partner.

5 WRITING

A Read the message Sofia sent to her college roommate Emma.

1. Are the underlined words correct or not? Find the three mistakes and correct them.

2. Answer the questions about Sofia:

   a. Where does Sofia live? How long has she been there?

   b. What does she do? How long has she had this job?

   c. Is Sofia married or dating anyone? If yes, how long have they been together?

Hey Emma,

How are you? <u>I haven't seen</u> you in a long time. What are you doing these days? A lot <u>has changed</u> for me <u>since</u> college. At the moment, I'm living in Barcelona. <u>I'm</u> here <u>since</u> three years, and I really like it. I came to Barcelona to go to graduate school. I <u>finished</u> three months ago, and I've just gotten a job at a local TV station. It's cool. In other news, I <u>haven't meet</u> anyone special, so I'm still single. What's new with you? Are you going to our class reunion next month? Let me know!

Sofia

Word Bank

Use *in other news* to change from talking about one topic to a different one.

At a *class reunion*, people from the same graduating class get together and have a party. Usually the people haven't seen each other for a long time.

B Imagine it's ten years in the future and you are doing something interesting in your life. Answer questions 2a–c in **A** about your future life. Use the present perfect tense. Then use your notes and the example to help you write an email to a classmate.

Park Güell, Barcelona

C 🔄 Exchange papers with a partner.

1. Circle any mistakes in your partner's email. Answer questions 2a–c in **A** about your partner.

2. Return the paper to your partner. Make corrections to your own email.

6 COMMUNICATION

A 🔀 Imagine it's ten years in the future and you are at a class reunion. Talk to six different people and find out what they're doing these days. Use your notes from Writing.

B 🔄 Think about the people at the reunion. Which of your classmates has changed the most? Tell a partner.

> So, what's new, Sofia?

> A lot. I'm living in Barcelona now.

> No way! How long have you been there?

2 BUSINESS AND MARKETING

Look at the photo. Answer the questions.

1 Where is this shopping district? What kinds of products are sold there?

2 How many advertisements do you see or hear every day? Where do you encounter them?

3 What is one advertisement that is popular now in your country?

UNIT GOALS

1 Describe and ask questions about companies

2 Emphasize important points

3 Give an opinion about different advertisements

4 Review a product

Colorful billboards advertise video games and other computer goods in a popular shopping area in Tokyo.

Bottles of Sriracha sauce

1 VIDEO Sriracha

A 🔄 Do you like spicy food? If so, what are your favorite dishes? If not, why not? Tell a partner.

B ▶ You are going to watch a video about spicy Sriracha sauce. Complete each sentence with a number from the box.

20	30	50	70	200,000
25	40	60	4,000	250,000

1. They make Sriracha sauce in a $ _____ million plant.

2. They produce _____ bottles of the sauce each day.

3. The main ingredient, jalapeno peppers, comes from a farm _____ miles away.

4. Farmer Craig Underwood has worked with David Tran for _____ years.

5. Tran started with just _____ acres (202,000 square meters) of land.

6. Next year he will have _____ acres (16.2 square kilometers).

7. There are more than _____ barrels in the warehouse.

8. Last year the company sold $ _____ million in sauce.

9. It's growing _____ % each year.

10. David Tran has worked on his product for more than _____ years.

C 🔄 What is the most interesting or surprising thing about David's story? Tell a partner.

2 VOCABULARY

A 🔁 Read the sentences. How many of the words in blue do you know? What do they mean? Use your dictionary to help you. Compare your answers with a partner's.

1. They plan to **advertise** their new product on TV and online.
2. If you **consume** too many calories, you'll gain weight.
3. Since our sales plan isn't working, we'll have to **develop** a new one.
4. Their company is pretty small. It only **employs** 20 people.
5. They are looking for someone to **invest** $2 million in the project.
6. Ms. Park is the head of that department. She **manages** ten people.
7. A: What does your company make?
   B: It **produces** batteries for phones.
8. My doctor **promotes** walking as a way to lose weight.
9. Do you want to buy something? To **purchase** an item, please click on the *Buy now* button.
10. Once we receive your money, we'll **ship** your order to you.

B Complete the chart with the noun forms of the verbs. Be careful of the spelling! Check your answers in a dictionary.

Nouns ending in *–ment*				Nouns ending in *–tion*	
advertise	advertisement	invest		consume	consumption
develop		manage		produce	
employ		ship		promote	

C 🔁 Make four questions using the words in **A** and **B**. Take turns asking the questions with a partner.

What have you purchased online recently?

I downloaded a couple of songs from iTunes.

How many people does Samsung employ?

I don't know, but since it's a large international company it's probably a large number.

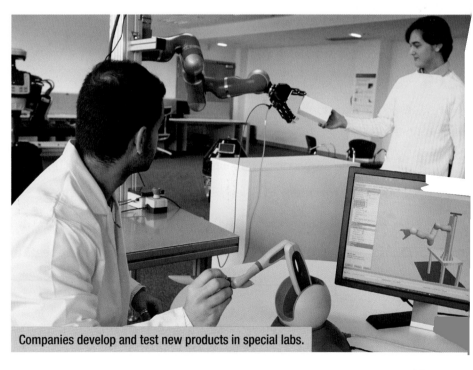

Companies develop and test new products in special labs.

3 LISTENING

A Circle the things that you do a lot. Where are you when you do these things?

send emails   watch videos   send text messages   talk on the phone

B 🔊 **Listen for the main idea.** Read the questions and responses below. Listen and circle the best answer to each question. **Track 7**

1. What is the main purpose of the article Lian is reading?
   a. to talk about how many hours we spend online
   b. to describe our Internet habits
   c. to give tips for using the Internet well
   d. to give solutions for Internet addiction

2. What does the article say about the two groups of people?
   a. Everyone wants to stay connected.
   b. They both get specific information online.
   c. They go online for different reasons.
   d. The number of people in both groups is increasing.

C 🔊 🔁 Listen again. Describe Arturo's and Lian's online behavior with a partner. How are they different? **Track 7**

D 🔊 **Listen for details; Identify a speaker.** What reasons does Arturo give to explain his behavior? Listen again and circle your answers. **Track 7**

1. He doesn't like social media.
2. He likes to know what's new.
3. He only goes online for specific reasons.
4. He wants to stay connected.

E 🔁 Are you more like Arturo or Lian? How so? Discuss with a partner.

F 🔊 **Pronunciation: Stress on nouns and verbs with the same spelling.** Listen and repeat the following sentences. Note where the stress falls in the underlined words. **Track 8**

NOUN: How many <u>PREsents</u> did you get for your birthday?
VERB: He <u>preSENTS</u> his ideas to the board at 2:00.

G 🔊 Practice saying these sentences. Then listen and repeat. **Track 9**

NOUN	VERB
1. a. What's your email <u>address</u>?	b. I need to <u>address</u> this package.
2. a. You should check the <u>record</u>.	b. You should try <u>recording</u> your hours.
3. a. There has been an <u>increase</u> in numbers.	b. The number of users is <u>increasing</u>.

4 SPEAKING

A 🔊 Complete the interview by filling in the missing questions. Write the correct numbers in the blanks. Then listen and check your answers.
Track 10

1. Can I get one of your audiobooks?
2. How exactly do you do that—put people first?
3. Maybe you've seen one of our advertisements online?
4. So, my first question is, what *does* Sound Smart do exactly?
5. What is the main focus of your company?
6. Where can I get an application?

HOST: I'd like to welcome Beverly Smith, the CEO for Sound Smart Inc., to our show today. Welcome, Beverly! _____

BEVERLY: Well, as you know, a lot of people are studying English. And many of them want to be able to study anywhere, so we produce audiobooks... _____

HOST: Yes, I have. What a great idea—how convenient! _____

BEVERLY: Sure. After you make a purchase, you can download the book online. It's simple.

HOST: _____

BEVERLY: Well, we really believe in our employees. The bottom line is that happy employees make a good product. So our company slogan is *People First!*

HOST: _____

BEVERLY: Well, for one thing, we have a lot of perks.* Our company has its own gym in the building. Also, each of our 100 employees gets the day off on his or her birthday.

HOST: Nice! _____

*perks = extra things you receive because of your job (for example, extra holidays, etc.)

B 🔄 Now cover the conversation in **A** and complete the company profile of Sound Smart with a partner.

Name of company: *Sound Smart*

Product / Service: _____

Company slogan: _____

Perks: _____

Other: _____

Useful Expressions
Asking about companies
What does your company do exactly?
What is the main focus of your company?
How do you...?
Emphasizing important points
I'd like to emphasize that...
Never forget that...
This is a key point.
The bottom line is...

SPEAKING STRATEGY

C 🔄 Work with a partner to create your own company. On a piece of paper, make a company profile.

D 🔄 You're going to tell another pair of students about your company. Prepare a short presentation with your partner. Use the Useful Expressions to help you emphasize certain points.

E 👥 Take turns presenting to another pair. The students who are listening should ask questions similar to those in **A**. Would you like to work for the company you heard about? Why or why not?

5 GRAMMAR

A Turn to pages 71–72. Complete the exercises. Then do **B–D** below.

The Passive Voice: Simple Present and Simple Past			
Subject	***be* + past participle**	***by* + object**	**Questions**
Audiobooks	**are made**	**by** Sound Smart.	Are audiobooks made by Sound Smart?
The company	**was founded**	**by** Beverly Smith.	How are the books made?

B Read these sentences about a neighborhood. Then rewrite each sentence as a passive sentence. Include the object where needed.

1. People settled this neighborhood 200 years ago.

   This neighborhood was _____

2. Everyone knows the neighborhood for its cute shops and boutiques.

   _____

3. They call the main shopping street Hoyt Street.

   _____

4. Merchants sell clothing and household goods.

   _____

5. The residents use many different forms of transportation to get around.

   _____

6. Some neighbors hold street fairs in the summer.

   _____

C 🔁 In which passive sentences in **B** did you include the object (*by* + noun)? Why did you leave the object out of the other sentences? Tell a partner.

D 🔁 Write questions in the passive for the statements in **B**. Then ask a partner those questions about his or her own neighborhood.

> When was your neighborhood settled?

> I'm not sure exactly, but I *do* know it's very old.

6 COMMUNICATION

A 🔄 Look at the map and photos. Then read about Iceland and answer the four questions with a partner.

1. Is Iceland a big or small country?
2. Is it hot or cold there?
3. What else do you know about Iceland?
4. How is it different from your country?

B 🔄 With a partner, state the different facts about Iceland. Use active and passive sentences. Use the verbs in the box in your description.

import / **export** (food, gas, products)
make / **produce** (cars, electronics)
find / **see** (natural wonders, wild animals)
grow (produce)
speak (languages)

> Many hot springs are found in Iceland.

> You can see polar bears there.

C 🔄 With a partner, make a list of facts about your city, region, or country. Use at least three of the verbs from the box in **B**. Present your list of facts to the class.

Iceland

Population: 330,000

Capital city: Reykjavik

Literacy rate: Almost 100%

Natural wonders: Glaciers, geysers, waterfalls, hot springs

Government: Democracy (the world's oldest)

Animals: Cattle, sheep, polar bears, seabirds

Produce: Turnips, potatoes

Exports: Seafood

Money: Icelandic krona

Languages: Icelandic, English, Nordic languages

Activities: Whale watching, hiking, skiing

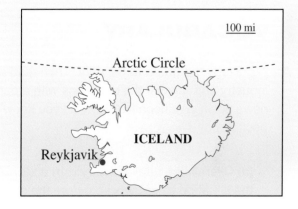

a glacier

a waterfall

A man makes trades on the stock market.

1 VOCABULARY

A ⟳ Study the graph at the right. Then read about the retail industry and answer the questions with a partner. Is most of the news positive or negative? How do you know? What is the positive news?

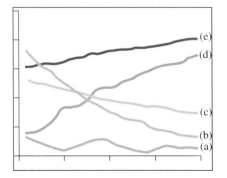

(a) Overall, the retail industry is **in a slump**. Experts expect the situation to **get worse** before the economy can **recover**. **Profits** continue to be **down**. (b) For the last few years, a number of companies have experienced a **sharp fall** in profits. Newspapers continue to struggle. (c) There has been a **steady decline** in in-store purchases for the third year in a row. But there is one bright spot in the news: (d) The number of retail companies advertising on the Internet has **increased dramatically**, and (e) overall consumer spending online has **risen slightly**.

Word Bank
in a slump = a period when the economy is not doing well
profits = income; money earned

B Use some of the words in **blue** to complete the chart.

	Adjectives	Adverbs
small in amount	slight	_____
constant, not sudden	gradual, _____	gradually, steadily
large in amount, sudden	dramatic, _____	_____, sharply

Verbs / Nouns
(↑) _____, _____
(↓) decrease, _____,
_____

C 🔄 Read about the graphs. Then use the words in the box to complete sentences about them. You will use one of the words twice. Compare your answers with a partner's.

decrease	gradual	rose	a slump
down	increase	slightly	up

1. We've seen a(n) _____ _____ in unemployment, but numbers are still _____.

2. New car sales are in _____. Recently they _____ _____.

3. The number of students studying English is _____ and ___*down*___, but overall there has been a(n) _____.

2 LISTENING

A 🔄 What is a commercial that you can remember? What do you remember most about it (the words, a character, a song)? Tell a partner.

B 🔊 **Take notes; Listen for specific information.** Listen to three commercials. What kind of product is advertised in each one? Write down key words you hear. **Track 11**

1. Product: _____

   Key words: _____

2. Product: _____

   Key words: _____

3. Product: _____

   Key words: _____

Word Bank
catchy = fun and easy to remember
clever = funny or interesting in a smart way
slogan = a short, easy-to-remember phrase used in an ad to sell a product

C 🔊 🔄 **Listen for gist.** Listen again. How did each ad try to make you buy the product? Circle the correct answer. Then explain your answers to a partner. **Track 11**

Ad 1: a. It told a moving story.

　　　b. It made a personal connection.

Ad 2: a. It talked about an innovative product.

　　　b. It had a catchy slogan.

Ad 3: a. It targeted specific people.

　　　b. It had a jingle.

D 🔄 Would you buy or use any of these products? Discuss with a partner.

3 READING 🔊 Track 12

A 🔁 Do you think advertising is necessary to sell products? Why or why not? Tell a partner.

B 🔁 **Identify a point of view; Draw conclusions.** Read the article. How would the author of the article answer the question in **A**? Use information from the article to explain your answer to a partner.

C **Scan for details.** Complete the sentences with the correct information.

1. Many people think that ads are a _____ influence.

2. The law in São Paulo took down over _____ billboards.

3. The ads in São Paulo covered _____ and _____ that needed to be cleaned.

4. The ads were replaced by _____.

5. One of the best ways to learn about new products is by _____ - _____ - _____, that is, from family and friends.

6. _____ reviews are a modern version of word-of-mouth.

D 🔁 Answer the questions with a partner.

1. Do you think it's a good idea to limit ads in public places, like they did in São Paulo?

2. Do you think that there are too many ads in your city?

3. Has an ad ever persuaded you to buy or do something?

4. Have you ever read online reviews of a product? Do you trust them? Why or why not?

LIFE **ADS?** YOU?

Is advertising really necessary? Billions of dollars are spent on it every year, so it must be important. After all, it's a busy world. You have to advertise to get people's attention to sell products!

But there is a downside to this. Researchers say that ads can negatively influence people to make them feel like they should be someone else. They argue that the ads are deceptive[1] and create a false sense of reality. Research has even shown that many children can't tell the difference between an ad and real life!

Others believe there are too many ads and that they make cities look unattractive. Some cities are taking action. In 2006, a law was passed in São Paulo, Brazil, that prohibited ads such as outdoor posters and billboards.[2] Over 15,000 billboards were taken down. This has caused people to look at their city in a new way. Before, their attention was constantly drawn to the large number of ads on

the streets. But now, people are able to clearly view and enjoy the beauty of the old buildings and modern structures.

In addition, problems that existed in the city for years are now getting fixed. For example, some neighborhoods needed to be cleaned and buildings needed to be repaired, but ads covered those areas and made them easy to ignore. When the billboards came down, people noticed the problems and started to fix them. Now these buildings are covered in beautiful art. São Paulo was one of the first major cities to pass a law like this, but now other cities, such as Paris, Tehran, and New York, have taken steps to reduce the number of advertisements on the streets.

So, how do people hear about new products now? One of the oldest, and best, ways is still word-of-mouth. People trust friends, family, and people they talk to more than they trust billboards. This makes word-of-mouth very persuasive![3] Word-of-mouth advertising has other advantages, too. It's cost-effective (after all, it's free), and a company doesn't have to create a complex business plan to do it.

Many people also use the Internet to review and share products. This is similar to word-of-mouth because people discuss opinions and personal experiences, but many more people can be part of the conversation. You have to be careful about online reviews, though. Unlike a suggestion from a friend or family member, you don't always know who is posting a review online!

[1]If something is *deceptive*, it makes you believe something that is not true.
[2]A *billboard* is a large ad on a sign.
[3]If something is *persuasive*, it makes someone believe something.

4 GRAMMAR

A Turn to page 73. Complete the exercises. Then do **B** and **C** below.

Connecting Ideas with *because, so, although / even though*	
She uses that product **Because** it's the cheapest,	**because** it's the cheapest. she uses that product.
This snack is 100% natural,	**so** a lot of moms buy it for their kids.
Many people buy that car **Even though** / **Although** it's expensive,	**even though** / **although** it's expensive. many people buy that car.

B With a partner, combine the sentences using *because, so,* or *although / even though*.

1. Female models in clothing ads are very thin. Girls want to be very thin.

   _____

2. Lottery ads show people winning a lot of money. Most people don't win any money.

   _____

3. Energy drinks are advertised on sites popular with teens. Teens buy more of these drinks.

   _____

4. A TV ad shows only boys playing with a popular toy. Girls like the toy, too.

   _____.

C Answer questions 1–4 below with a partner. Use *so, because, although,* and *even though* to explain your opinions.

Should…

1. very thin models be used in clothing ads for women?
2. lottery ads be shown on TV?
3. energy drinks be advertised on sites popular with teens?
4. some toys be advertised to boys (or girls) only?

> Even though it's important to look good, the girls in clothing ads are too thin. It's not healthy.

> I agree, so I don't shop at those stores.

5 WRITING

A Read the product review. Answer the questions with a partner.

1. What product is the person reviewing?
2. What are the good and bad things about it?
3. Does the person give the product a mostly positive or negative review?

B Think of something you bought recently. What are the positive and negative things about this product? Make notes. Then use your ideas and the example to help you write a product review.

THIS PRODUCT IS RATED: ★★★★★

I like to go mountain biking. When it's hot, I need to drink a lot of water. I like to use my Hydro-Pak because I can ride and drink at the same time! The Hydro-Pak is convenient and lightweight, and it comes in many different colors. Although it's more expensive than other models, it definitely is the best!

C  Exchange your writing with a partner. Read his or her review.

1. Are there any mistakes? If yes, circle them.

2. Answer the questions in **A** about your partner's product. Do you know this product? Do you agree with your partner's review?

3. Return the paper to your partner. Make corrections to your own review.

4. Publish a collection of class product reviews.

6 COMMUNICATION

The Citybike Mini: "The Foldable Bike"

Pros: It's...

• lightweight.

• easy to store at school or work.

• easy to carry on public transportation.

Cons: It's...

• expensive.

• only good for short bike rides.

A  You and your partner work for an advertising agency. You need to create a minute-long commercial for TV or the Internet for the product above. On a piece of paper, write your ideas. As you create the ad, think about the questions below. Then practice doing your commercial.

1. Does the ad have a catchy slogan or song?

_____

2. Which word(s) best describe(s) the ad; circle your choice(s):

moving   clever   inspiring   other: _____

3. Is the ad persuasive? Would you buy the product after watching the ad? Why or why not?

_____

B  Get together with another pair and perform your commercial for them. When you watch, answer questions 1–3 in **A**. Then explain your answers to the presenters using *because*, *so*, and *even though / although*.

> Even though the ad was clever, I don't think people would buy the bike because...

3 OUR WORLD

Divers swim with humpback whales
off the coast of Mexico.

Look at the photo. Answer the questions.

1 What animals are in the photo? What do you know about them?

2 What are the people doing? Why do you think they are doing this?

3 What is one way that humans might be affecting these animals and their natural habitat?

UNIT GOALS

1 Describe rare animals and their habitats

2 Ask questions in an indirect way

3 Offer another opinion

4 Talk about man-made structures and their impact on the environment

Walter Fuller walks down Ormond Beach, California.

1 VIDEO The Steward of Ormond Beach

A Read the title. What is a *steward*? What do you think a steward of a beach does?

B ▶ Watch the video. Circle *True* or *False* for each item.

1. Walter Fuller is the steward for Ormond Beach.	True	False
2. His other title is "protector of sea life of Ormond."	True	False
3. For the past 15 years, Walter has been living at Ormond Beach.	True	False
4. In the beginning, Walter visited the beach on his days off.	True	False
5. There are many wetland areas on the Southern California coast.	True	False
6. Walter used to be a volunteer.	True	False
7. In high school, Walter studied the eagle family.	True	False
8. The coastline is considered to be a beautiful part of the United States.	True	False
9. Walter says that having a job motivates him.	True	False

C 🗘 Answer these questions. Share your answers with a partner.

1. What area do you know that needs a steward? _____

2. Why did you choose that area?

2 VOCABULARY

A ⟳ Work with a partner. You are going to learn about two different animals. Follow the instructions below. Look up any words you don't know.

Student A: Read the information about **snow leopards**.

Student B: Read the information about **mountain gorillas**.

Snow leopards	Mountain gorillas
We don't know exactly how many snow leopards there are, but we do know their numbers are **declining**. Today, there may be as few as 3,000 **in the wild**.	Mountain gorillas live in **dense** forests. They can climb trees, but spend most of their time on the ground.
The secretive animals live in the countries of Central Asia, but people **rarely** see them.	They are found in Africa—in Rwanda and Congo.
They have thick fur that helps them survive the cold winters of their mountain **environment**.	The gorillas are **endangered** (currently only 900 **remain**) due to **illegal** hunting and loss of their **habitat**.
The leopards like to eat sheep and goats, and for this reason, many are killed by sheepherders.	Even so, their numbers are slowly **increasing** because they are **protected**.

B ⟳ Interview your partner about his or her animal. Ask questions to complete the information in the chart.

	Snow leopard	**Mountain gorilla**
Population		
Habitat		
Location		
Challenges		

> How many snow leopards are there?

C ⟳ The snow leopard and the mountain gorilla are **suffering**. Both animals are almost **extinct**. What would you do to **raise awareness** of their situations? What would you tell people? Discuss with a partner.

3 LISTENING

A 🔄 **Use background knowledge.** Look at the photo. What animal is this? What do you know about it? Discuss with a partner.

B 🔊 **Listen for details.** Listen to four descriptions of animals that live in the rainforest. Circle the correct words to complete the definitions. **Track 13**

Listening 1   *Rodent* means dog / rat.
               To exceed means to be greater / lesser than (an amount).

Listening 2   *Snout* means nose / legs.
               Nocturnal means active / inactive at night.

Listening 3   *To camouflage* means to escape / to hide.
               To inhabit means to eat / to live.

Listening 4   *An acrobat* does tricks on the ground / in the air.
               To leap means to jump / to fall.

C 🔊 **Listen for numbers.** Listen again. Complete the sentences with the numbers in the box. Three numbers are extra. **Track 13**

1	1.12	1.2	5	12	66	68	135	138	180

Capybara   1. can hold its breath underwater for up to _____ minute(s)

                       2. can weigh up to _____ kilo(s)

                       3. can be more than _____ meter(s) long

Tapir   4. weighs between _____ and _____ kilo(s)

Sloth   5. comes down to the ground _____ time(s) a week

Spider monkey   6. can jump over _____ meter(s)

D Look at the photo in **A** again. What animal is it?
How do you know?

4 SPEAKING

A 🔊 Gustav and Carolina are telling Bart about their summer job. Listen to and read their conversation. Where did they work and what did they do? Why can't Bart apply for the job?
Track 14

BART: So, what exactly did you do over the summer?

GUSTAV: We worked as volunteers at Glacier National Park.

BART: I've never been there. What's it like?

CAROLINA: It's beautiful. There are mountains and lakes... and, of course, glaciers!

BART: How was the job?

GUSTAV: We had to do a lot of physical work. It was kind of hard.

CAROLINA: That's true, but it was exciting, too! We actually saw bears!

BART: Wow! That *does* sound exciting. Maybe I should apply. I'll need a job next summer.

CAROLINA: Sorry, Bart, but you can't apply to that program. It's a special program for international students.

B 👥 Practice the conversation in groups of three.

SPEAKING STRATEGY

C 🔁 Imagine that you and your partner are looking for a place to live together as roommates. Write down some of the important things to consider.

cost, _____

_____

_____

Useful Expressions
Offering another opinion
That's true, but...
Yes, but on the other hand,...
Even so,...
But then again,...

D 🔁 Read about these two possible places to live. Add three more ideas to each list. With a partner, discuss the positive and negative aspects of each place. Use the Useful Expressions to help you.

City apartment	Suburban home
expensive	big backyard
near public transportation	need a car
small bedrooms	quiet neighborhood
big balcony with a great view	nothing to do on weekends
_____	_____
_____	_____
_____	_____

> An apartment in the city would be expensive.

> Yes, but on the other hand, living in the city is exciting. There's so much to do!

E 👥 With your partner, have a discussion and then choose one of the places to live in **D**. Tell the class which location you chose and why.

5 GRAMMAR

A Turn to pages 74–75. Complete the exercises. Then do **B–D** below.

Embedded Questions	
What is a tapir?	Do you know **what a tapir is**? I'd like to know **what a tapir is**.
Asking for information	**Saying you don't know something**
Can / Could you tell me… Do you know… Do you remember… Do you have any idea…	I don't know / I'd like to know… I'm not sure… I can't remember… I wonder…

B Find and correct the error in each sentence.

1. Could you tell me what is the answer?

2. Can you remember me how to get there?

3. I'm not sure how to do it?

4. What's your opinion? I like to know what you think.

5. I'm not sure where is the exit.

C Turn each question on the left into an embedded question on the right.

1. Where do they live?   I'd like to _____ where _____.

2. What is their habitat?   Can you _____ me _____?

3. What challenges do they face?   Do you _____ any _____ what _____?

4. How much does a capybara weigh?   I'm not _____ how much _____.

5. How do sloths sleep?   I wonder _____.

6. Where do tapirs spend their time?   I don't know _____.

7. Why are monkeys called "acrobats"?   Do you know _____?

8. What is the name of that animal?   I can't _____ what _____.

D Think of an animal. Take turns asking a partner about his or her animal.

> Can you tell me where red pandas live?

> They're from China.

> What is their habitat?

> I'm not sure what their habitat is. Maybe they live in the mountains.

6 COMMUNICATION

A Work alone. Take the quiz. Look up any words you don't know.

A *harbor* is a protected area of water where boats are protected from storms.

What / Where is the world's...

1. busiest harbor?
   a. Singapore
   b. Pusan (South Korea)
   c. Hong Kong (China)

2. largest island?
   a. Great Britain
   b. Greenland (Denmark)
   c. Honshu (Japan)

3. highest waterfall?
   a. Tugela Falls (South Africa)
   b. Angel Falls (Venezuela)
   c. Sutherland Falls (New Zealand)

4. oldest active volcano?
   a. Kilauea (US)
   b. Yasur (Vanuatu)
   c. Etna (Italy)

5. longest mountain range?
   a. the Austrian Alps (Europe)
   b. the Andes (South America)
   c. the Urals (Europe)

6. longest cave?
   a. Mammoth Cave (US)
   b. Holloch Cave (Switzerland)
   c. Sistema Ox Bel Ha (Mexico)

7. deepest lake?
   a. Lake Superior (US / Canada)
   b. Lake Nyasa (Africa)
   c. Lake Baikal (Russia)

8. largest desert?
   a. the Sahara (North Africa)
   b. the Australian (Australia)
   c. the North American (Mexico / US)

9. longest coastline?
   a. Australia
   b. Canada
   c. Chile

B Get into a group of four people. Imagine that you are on a quiz show. Follow the steps below.

> Maria, do you know what the largest island in the world is?

> I'm not sure what the answer is, but I chose Great Britain. Is that correct?

Student A: quiz show announcer

Students B–D: quiz show contestants

1. **Student A:** Read a question from the quiz in **A**.

2. **Students B–D:** Write down your answer on a piece of paper.

3. **Student A:** Ask each contestant for his or her answer. Then check page 82 and give each contestant one point for a correct answer. Continue asking questions.

4. **Students B–D:** The person with the most points at the end of the game wins.

The Burj Khalifa, Dubai, United Arab Emirates

- This skyscraper is the tallest building in the world at 829.8 meters (2,722 feet).

- Architects **proposed** ideas for the building in 2003 and **construction** was finished in 2010.

- Architects faced many **obstacles** in building a skyscraper this big. The building needed to be very strong to **withstand** its own weight! The extreme heat of Dubai also had to be **considered**.

- Another issue was how to safely and quickly **transport** people and **goods** around the building. The builders found an **efficient** solution to **get around** this problem. The building has 57 high-speed elevators. Each can travel 600 meters a minute and **accommodate** 10–12 people.

- The building has many **sustainable** features as well. For example, it collects and reuses water from the air conditioners, saving 15 million gallons of water a year!

1 VOCABULARY

A 🔄 What do you know about the famous building in this photo? Tell a partner. Then take turns reading about it aloud.

B 🔄 Complete the sentences using the words in **blue** from above. Work with a partner.

1. Engineers need to make sure the skyscraper can ____withstand____ earthquakes before they start _____.

2. There are other _____ to think about, too. For example, where will people park?

3. To answer this question, the architect _____ an idea: build an underground parking lot. It will be able to _____ 1,500 cars.

4. From the parking lot, an elevator will _____ people and goods to the top floor in 15 seconds.

5. The team _____ the architect's idea and agreed with his suggestion.

6. There should also be a(n) _____ way of heating and cooling the building.

7. With solar panels, the building will have plenty of energy and also be _____.

C 🔄 Discuss the questions with a partner.

1. Why is the Burj Khalifa special?

2. What were some of the obstacles that architects faced when they designed it?

3. What's special about the building's elevators?

4. How is the building good for the environment?

2 LISTENING

A Which words in the box do you know? With a partner, look up any unfamiliar words in your dictionary.

architect	edge	investigate
blueprint	get access (to a place)	leaky

B **Listen for gist.** Which photo shows what the woman does in her job? Listen and circle the correct one. **Track 15**

C **Listen for details.** Listen. Complete the sentences about Jamie's job. **Track 15**

1. Jamie works with _____ buildings.

2. She checks problems so that they don't _____ mistakes.

3. Rappelling is a way to get access to _____ places.

4. After you hook up to the top of the building, you _____ over the edge.

5 Rappelling is scary, but you can get _____.

D **Pronunciation: Negative questions to confirm information.** Complete the negative questions. Then listen and check your answers. **Track 16**

1. (be / you / an engineer) _Aren't you an engineer?_   That's correct. I'm a civil engineer.

2. (work / you / on the second floor) _____   No, actually I work on the third floor.

3. (be / the Burj Khalifa / in the UAE) _____   Yes, it is, in Dubai.

4. (be / the Eiffel Tower / built in 1900) _____   No. It was finished in 1889.

E Practice asking and answering questions 1–4 in **D** with a partner. Pay attention to intonation.

A **Use background knowledge; Make predictions.** Look at the title and the names of the two countries in the article. Do you know anything about these countries? What do you think is happening in these countries?

B **Take notes on key details.** Read the article. As you read, think about questions 1 and 2. Underline the information in the passage that answers the questions.

1. How are rising sea levels affecting the Seychelles and the Netherlands specifically?

2. What is each country doing about these problems?

C **Infer meaning.** Match the words in bold in the reading with their definitions.

_____ a short description

_____ planned pieces of work

_____ to damage land or rock so it disappears

_____ close to the height of the ocean

_____ walls built across bodies of water to hold the water back

D 🔁 **Summarize; Give opinions.** Answer the questions with a partner.

1. Look again at the questions in **B**. Explain your answers to a partner in your own words.

2. Has global warming affected the area where you live? What do you think can be done to help?

WHEN THE SEAS RISE

A solar-powered floating house in Rotterdam, the Netherlands.

When most people think of global warming[1], they think of something that will happen in the future, something that doesn't affect their daily life. But for many people around the world, the future is now. Research shows that sea levels worldwide have been rising at a rate of 0.14 inches (3.5 millimeters) per year since the early 1990s. The trend, linked to global warming, is putting thousands of coastal cities at risk of being destroyed over time. The two countries below offer a **snapshot** of what climate change might look like for all of us.

Seychelles

This chain of islands in the Indian Ocean has been called one of the most beautiful places on Earth. There is a problem, though. Many of the country's most populated regions were constructed in **low-lying** areas, near the water. As sea levels rise, many people will lose their homes.

Already, the island's tourism industry is being hurt. Seychelles's famous beaches are being **eroded** by the rising water, as well as by storms that grow more powerful each year. In addition, the country's coral reefs (a popular tourist attraction) are suffering because of warmer water.

To fight these problems, the government of the Seychelles has been trying to relocate people living in low-lying coastal areas to higher ground. Unfortunately, there isn't enough land to accommodate many of these people. The country's citizens are also trying to bring as much attention as possible to global warming and the danger it poses. They point out that if these things happen to the Seychelles, they can happen to big countries like the United States, China, or Brazil next.

The Netherlands

For the people of the Netherlands, rising waters have been an obstacle for years. The country is close to 30 percent under sea level! A series of **dams and dikes** has protected the country from mass flooding for many years, but as sea levels continue to rise, more extreme solutions are being considered. One of them is a large increase in "floating houses." These houses are built on water or in areas that flood, and each structure is able to rise and fall with the water. Sustainable and efficient apartment buildings that can float are also being planned.

Engineers in the Netherlands are also continuing the country's tradition of doing large construction **projects** to help hold the water back. Larger dams have been built in recent years, and rivers have been rerouted so they are not as close to cities. Today, engineers from many countries visit the Netherlands to learn more about these projects. They fear that in the future, as the Earth warms and sea levels continue to rise, Dutch building techniques will have to be used all over the world.

[1]*Global warming* is an increase in the Earth's temperature, caused in part by humans' use of fossil fuels (oil, gas). As the Earth warms, ice melts, causing sea levels to rise.

4 GRAMMAR

A Turn to pages 75–76. Complete the exercises. Then do **B** below.

The Passive with Various Tenses		
	Active	**Passive**
Simple present	Engineers <u>build</u> skyscrapers with a steel frame structure.	Most skyscrapers **are built** with a steel frame structure.
Simple past	The Woolworth Company <u>built</u> a skyscraper in 1913.	One of the first skyscrapers **was built** in 1913.
Present perfect	Engineers <u>have built</u> the world's tallest building in Dubai.	The world's tallest building **has been built** in Dubai.
Present continuous	Engineers <u>are building</u> a lot of tall buildings in Shanghai.	A lot of tall buildings **are being built** in Shanghai.
Simple future	Someday they <u>will build</u> a skyscraper without concrete.	Someday a skyscraper without concrete **will be built**.

B 🔗 Work with a partner. Follow the steps below.

1. Read the information below. Look up the underlined words in a dictionary.

2. Each person should choose a role (Student A or B).

3. Debate the issue with your partner. In your own words, explain what you want to do. Give two reasons to support your opinion. Try to agree about what to do.

4. Share your plan with another pair.

A large construction company wants to <u>tear down</u> traditional buildings in a neighborhood in your city. The buildings are beautiful, but they were built 100 years ago and aren't in good condition.

Student A: You work for the construction company. Here is your plan:

- The old buildings will be torn down, and new office and apartment buildings will be built.

- The new buildings will be safer and will be able to accommodate more people.

- Former <u>tenants</u> will be allowed to move back into a new apartment, but it will take three years for the project to be finished. For now, those people must find other housing.

Student B: You live in one of the old buildings now. You have this opinion:

- A lot of modern buildings have been built in our city. Older structures should be <u>preserved</u>.

- Many people in the buildings are elderly. They shouldn't be <u>forced</u> to leave their homes.

> The old buildings should be preserved. They connect us with our past.

> Yes, but on the other hand, these old buildings may not withstand...

5 WRITING

A What do you think about the issue in Grammar **B**? In five minutes, outline your ideas below. Then, in 20 minutes, write a paragraph. Explain each reason with an extra sentence or two.

In my opinion, the old buildings should / shouldn't be torn down for two reasons.

For one thing, _____.

In addition, _____.

For these reasons, I believe the old buildings should / shouldn't be torn down.

B Exchange your writing with a partner. Circle any mistakes in your partner's writing. Do you agree with your partner's opinion? Why or why not? Return the paper to your partner. Make corrections to your own paragraph.

6 COMMUNICATION

A Read about Diamond City's problems. What projects have been proposed to solve these problems? Use your own words to explain each situation with a partner.

Problem 1: The dam was built 30 years ago, and it is weak.	**Problem 3:** The traffic is terrible, and businesses are leaving the city because of it.
Project: Repair the dam. This will take three years.	**Project:** Build a new subway line to transport people. It will take three years to finish.
Notes: The city has been hit by a huge flood every 100 years. The last flood was 20 years ago, and the downtown area was destroyed.	**Notes:** Construction will be difficult and expensive, but a new subway system is needed to transport people.
Problem 2: The baseball stadium is old.	**Problem 4:** There isn't enough office space in Diamond City.
Project: Repair the stadium. It will take two years.	**Project:** Build a new skyscraper to keep businesses in the city. It will take two years to finish.
Notes: The Diamond City Miners baseball team is a big moneymaker for the city. But if the stadium isn't fixed soon, the team may move to another city.	**Notes:** The land around the skyscraper is polluted and must be cleaned up first. This will take a year or more. Then construction can begin.

B With your partner, rank the projects in the order you would do them. Give reasons for your order. Note: A new project can be started only after the previous one has been finished.

C Explain your plan from **B** to another pair. Are your ideas similar? If not, whose plan is better? Why?

4 SOCIAL ISSUES

Look at the photo. Answer the questions.

1 What problems do you see in the photo?

2 Do these things happen where you live?

3 What is an important social issue (problem) where you live?

UNIT GOALS

1 Give a short formal presentation

2 State the purpose and important points of your presentation

3 Discuss environmental and social problems

4 Make predictions and talk about consequences

Traffic in downtown Bangkok, Thailand

Apartment buildings in Hong Kong, one of the *megacities* of the world.

1 **VIDEO** Seven Billion

A Currently, over 7 billion people live on Earth, and the number is increasing. Do you think this is a problem? Why or why not? Discuss with a partner.

B Work with a partner. Read the questions and guess the answers. Then watch the video to check your guesses.

1. It would take 2 / 20 / 200 years just to count to 7 billion out loud.

2. In 2045, the world's population could be 9 / 12 / 15 billion.

3. In 2010, the average person lived 53 / 61 / 69 years.

4. In 1960, the average person lived 53 / 61 / 69 years.

5. In 1975, the world's three megacities were New York City, Tokyo, and Mexico City / Rome / Sydney.

6. Right now there are 7 / 14 / 21 megacities in the world.

7. By 2050, 50 / 70 / 90% of us will be living in cities.

8. Seven billion people, speaking 7,000 languages, living in 19 / 94 / 194 countries.

C Read these statistics from the end of the video. Which one is the biggest problem and why? Discuss with a partner.

5% of the population consumes 23% of the world's energy.

13% of the people in the world don't have clean drinking water.

38% of the world's population lacks adequate sanitation.

2 VOCABULARY

A 🔁 Doris Chavez and Amelia Smith are running for mayor. Read their ads. Then answer the questions by checking the correct box(es) with a partner.

DORIS CHAVEZ for mayor!

"We're making progress in many areas.
Why change now? Reelect Doris Chavez!"

In her first term, Mayor Chavez:
- **launched** a new school lunch program for elementary school students.
- **taxed** large companies to raise extra money.
- **worked** enthusiastically to improve life for everyone—crime is down 30%.

There is no better candidate than
Doris Chavez for mayor!

AMELIA SMITH for mayor! ★ ★ ★ ★ ★

"No more politics as usual.
It's time for change in our city!
Vote for Amelia Smith!"

Amelia Smith vows:
- to **expand** the school lunch program to include older students.
- not to **raise taxes** on **corporations**.
- to work hard for all **citizens** to keep our city streets safe.

★ ★ ★ ★ ★ ★ ★ ★ ★ ★ ★ ★ ★ ★ ★ ★ ★

Amelia Smith is the clear choice for mayor!

	Doris	Amelia
1. Who is currently the mayor?	☐	☐
2. Who doesn't want to increase taxes?	☐	☐
3. Who is interested in the school lunch program?	☐	☐
4. Who mentions crime and safety?	☐	☐

B Look at the information in **A**. Write the word(s) in **blue** next to their definitions.

1. doing (something) the same way: _____as usual_____
2. eagerly, with great energy: _____
3. a fixed period of time: _____
4. increase in size: _____
5. large companies: _____
6. started: _____
7. promises: _____
8. moving forward: _____
9. obvious: _____
10. a person who is competing for a position: _____
11. members of a city or country: _____
12. made someone pay money to the government: _____

C 🔁 Discuss the questions with a partner.

1. Do you ever see ads like the ones in **A**? How else do politicians campaign where you live?
2. Think of a person who was up for reelection recently. Did people vote for or against him or her? Why?

3 LISTENING

A **Use background knowledge.** Read the sentences below. What does the word in bold mean? When do election campaigns typically happen?

There are two candidates running for mayor. The **campaign** will begin on February 1st, and the election will be on March 15th.

B 🔊 **Listen for gist.** Listen to the beginning of speeches given by Doris and Amelia. Choose the best answer to complete each sentence. (One answer is extra.) **Track 18**

1. Doris is giving her speech because _____

2. Amelia is giving her speech because _____

    a. she is going to run for mayor.

    b. she has been elected mayor.

    c. she has lost the race for mayor.

C 🔊 **Listen for context.** Listen again. Choose the best answers. **Track 18**

1. When Doris says *never in my wildest dreams*, she means...

    a. she was pretty sure.

    b. she couldn't imagine it.

2. When Doris says *I gave it my best shot*, she means...

    a. she was very disappointed.

    b. she worked really hard.

3. When Amelia says *Doris and I were running neck and neck*, she means...

    a. they had almost the same number of votes.

    b. there was a clear winner.

4. When Amelia says *we saw a record turnout*, she means...

    a. a large number of people voted.

    b. a small number of people voted.

D 🔊 🔁 **Listen for main ideas.** Now listen to the rest of Amelia's speech. Check (✓) the topics she refers to in her speech. What key words in the listening helped you choose your answers? Tell a partner. **Track 19**

☐ the economy ☐ public transportation ☐ crime ☐ pollution ☐ education

E 🔁 Look at the topics in **D**. Which one do you think is the biggest problem where you live? Why? Tell a partner.

Pollution is a major problem for many cities.

4 SPEAKING

A 🔊 Listen to and read the speech below. What is the problem? What is one thing causing it? Can you think of other causes? **Track 20**

Today I'd like to talk to you about rush hour traffic. I'll begin by telling you about the problem. Then I'll list the three things I think are causing this problem.

So, let's start by talking about rush hour traffic in this city. We've all experienced it, and in recent years it's gotten worse. Ten years ago, it used to take about 45 minutes to drive across town. Now it takes two hours. One of the main causes of this problem is too many cars on the road. More cars means more traffic and, of course, more traffic accidents. Another cause of rush hour traffic is...

B 🔊 **Pronunciation: Using pauses in public speaking.** Read the sentences below. Guess where the speaker will pause. Write a slash mark (/) for each pause. Then listen and check your answers. **Track 21**

What is one of the biggest problems facing our city today? It's rush hour traffic.

Today we're going to talk about this important problem. I'll begin by telling you about the problem. Then I'll list three things...

C 🔊 🔁 Listen again to the speech in **A** and take turns saying it aloud with a partner. Pay attention to pausing. **Track 20**

SPEAKING STRATEGY

D Match each word on the left with one on the right to make a list of common city problems. Write them on a piece of paper. Can you add to the list?

unaffordable	high		streets	unemployment
dirty	noise		housing	pollution

E 🔁 Choose one of the city problems in **D** or one of your own. Work with a partner and complete the information below.

Problem: _____

Causes of the problem:

1. _____

2. _____

3. _____

Useful Expressions: Language for presentations
Stating the purpose
Today, I'd like to talk to you about...
I'll begin by (talking about the issue). / I'll provide an overview of (the issue).
Then I'll list the (two / three / four)...
Stating important points
Let's talk first about... / Let's start by talking about...
One of the main causes of (traffic) is...
Another / A second cause of (traffic) is...
And finally...

F 👥 Join another pair and follow the instructions. Then switch roles and repeat.

Presenters: Use the Useful Expressions to explain your problem in **E** clearly. One person should introduce the talk. The second person should explain the causes of the problem.

Listeners: Take notes. After the presentation, give suggestions for how to solve the problem.

5 GRAMMAR

A Turn to pages 77–78. Complete the exercises. Then do **B–D** below.

Too + Adjective / Adverb; *too much* / *too many* + Noun				
	too	**Adjective / adverb**	**(Infinitive)**	
You're 17. You're	**too**	young	to vote.	
I can't understand him. He speaks	**too**	quickly.		
	too much / too many	**Noun**	**(Infinitive)**	
	Too much	pollution		is bad for your lungs.
Our city has	**too many**	problems	to solve	in one day.

Adjective / Adverb + *enough*; *enough* + Noun				
	Adjective / adverb	***enough***	**(Infinitive)**	
I'm 21. I'm	old	**enough**	to vote.	
These are good seats. I can hear	well	**enough.**		
	enough	**Noun**	**(Infinitive)**	
We have	**enough**	water	to get by	for now.
They have	**enough**	police officers		on the street.

B Complete the statements about school life with *too, too much, too many,* and *enough*.

School Life	Agree	Disagree
1. There are _____ rules in this school.	☐	☐
2. There is _____ emphasis on memorization.	☐	☐
3. We don't have _____ time for extracurricular activities.	☐	☐
4. Classes are not interesting _____.	☐	☐
5. _____ students study only to pass the test.	☐	☐
6. We don't have _____ opportunities to practice English conversation.	☐	☐
7. There's _____ homework.	☐	☐
8. The school day is _____ long.	☐	☐

C Now check (✓) *Agree* or *Disagree* for each statement in **B**.

D 🔁 Share your answers with a partner. Give examples and discuss solutions for the statements you agreed with.

> I think there are too many rules in this school. For example, we shouldn't have to wear school uniforms all the time.

> I agree. I think you can look neat enough in a pair of jeans and a nice shirt.

6 COMMUNICATION

A Follow the instructions to complete the survey below. Then check (✓) *Yes* or *No*.

- **For questions 1–6:** Write *enough* before or after each word. (Only one position is correct.)
- **For questions 7–12:** Write *too*, *too much*, or *too many*.

	Yes	No
1. Did you get _____ sleep _____ last night?		
2. Do you have _____ credits _____ to graduate?		
3. Is it _____ quiet _____ for you to study at home?		
4. Do you typically have _____ time _____ to finish your homework?		
5. Have you eaten _____ food _____ today?		
6. Do you get along _____ well _____ with your parents?		
7. Do you spend _____ time watching TV?		
8. Is English _____ difficult to learn?		
9. Do you sometimes eat _____ sweets?		
10. Do you have _____ problems in your life?		
11. Is it possible to earn _____ money?		
12. At 20, are people _____ young to get married?		

B 🔁 Use the questions in **A** to interview a partner. Ask follow-up questions.

> Is it quiet enough for you to study at home?

> No, not really. It's pretty noisy.

> Where do you study then?

> Mostly at the library.

Suzzallo Library at the University of Washington in the United States

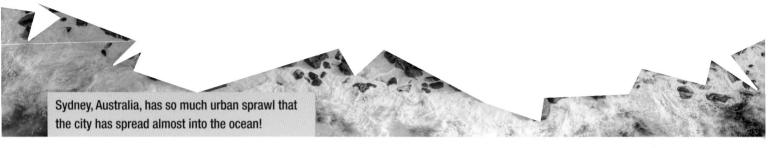

Sydney, Australia, has so much urban sprawl that the city has spread almost into the ocean!

1 VOCABULARY

A 🔁 Read about the problem of **sprawl**. Then tell a partner: Is sprawl a problem in your area?

- Sprawl is a problem in my city. In the past five years, there has been a lot of new **development**. As this **spreads** across the land, it **destroys** parks, farms, and open spaces.

- In many of these new neighborhoods, people live far away from public transportation, stores, and schools. This **forces** people to **rely on** their cars so they can drive longer distances. Driving a lot is a **waste** of time. It also creates more pollution.

- So what can we do? First, we should stop all new development. This will **protect** our open spaces for future generations. Then, we should **support** a law that **provides** money for public transportation and new bike paths. This will **encourage** people to leave their cars at home. If this happens, air quality will **improve**.

B Write a **blue** word from **A** next to its definition.

1. ___encourage___: to persuade or get someone to do something

2. _____: to damage completely

3. _____: to keep something safe

4. _____: to move gradually outward

5. _____: to use something in a bad or careless way

6. _____: to try to help a person or idea succeed

7. _____: to offer or give something

8. _____: to make someone do something difficult

9. _____: the building of houses, stores, and other structures

10. _____: to need or depend on something

11. _____: to make better

C 🔁 Answer the questions with your partner using the new words in **A**.

1. What is the problem with sprawl? What does it do?

2. What does the writer suggest doing? How will these things help?

2 LISTENING

A ♻ Look at the photos. Do you live in an urban or suburban area? Explain to a partner.

urban

suburban

B 🔊 **Listen for details; Infer information.** You will hear three speakers. Where do they live now? Where do they want to live in the future? Write *U* for urban and *S* for suburban. Write *NM* if the information is not mentioned. **Track 22**

Bella: now: _____   Anne: now: _____   Mercedes: now: _____

     future: _____   future: _____   future: _____

C 🔊 **Listen for reasons.** Where does each person want to live? Circle the answers below. Then listen and take notes on their reasons. **Track 23**

1. Bella wants to live in the city / suburbs.   Reason(s): _____

2. Anne wants to live in the city / suburbs.   Reason(s): _____

3. Mercedes wants to live in the city / suburbs.   Reason(s): _____

D ♻ What do you think the underlined expressions mean? Which person from **B** do you think would say each sentence? Write the names. Explain your answers to a partner.

1. I hope I can move—I have to <u>wait and see</u>, I guess.   _____

2. Now that I've <u>put down roots</u>, I probably won't move.   _____

3. I needed <u>a change of scenery</u>, and I got it!   _____

E ♻ Where do you want to live in the future? Why? Tell a partner.

3 READING 🔊 Track 24

A 🔄 **Use background knowledge.** This article is about a *daycare center* and a *retirement home*. What are these places? How are they similar? Discuss with a partner.

B 🔄 **Make predictions; Infer information.** Look at the photo. Answer the questions with a partner.

1. How do you think the people in the photo know each other?

2. Look at the word *intergenerational* in the caption. What do you think it means?

C **Infer meaning.** Read the article. Then match the words (1–4) with the correct definitions (a–d).

1. at risk (line 4) _____

2. launched (line 11) _____

3. be exposed to (line 31–32) _____

4. tolerant (line 34) _____

a. started

b. in danger of something bad happening

c. be given the chance to experience something new

d. able to accept different ideas and situations

D 🔄 **Read for details; Draw conclusions.** The article talks about an intergenerational program. What are the benefits of the program? Underline them in the passage. Can you think of any challenges? Explain your ideas to a partner.

E 🔄 Why do you think many older and younger people are in retirement homes and daycare centers in the US? Is this common in your country? Do you think it's good? Why or why not? Discuss with a partner.

PEOPLE OF ALL AGES

Did you know that in the United States, over 25 percent of senior citizens (people over 65) live alone? Without enough friends and family nearby, seniors are at risk for depression.[1]

5 This is a serious problem. Studies show that people with depression are more likely to have other health problems as well.

Now, many communities are trying to find a solution to this problem. Providence Mount 10 St. Vincent, a retirement home near Seattle, Washington, has recently launched an intergenerational program. Over 400 senior citizens live at Providence Mount St. Vincent, and over 40 children from a few months old 15 to age five go to daycare there. The children spend the day there with the senior citizens while workers look on.

[1]A person with *depression* feels very unhappy and unable to do anything.

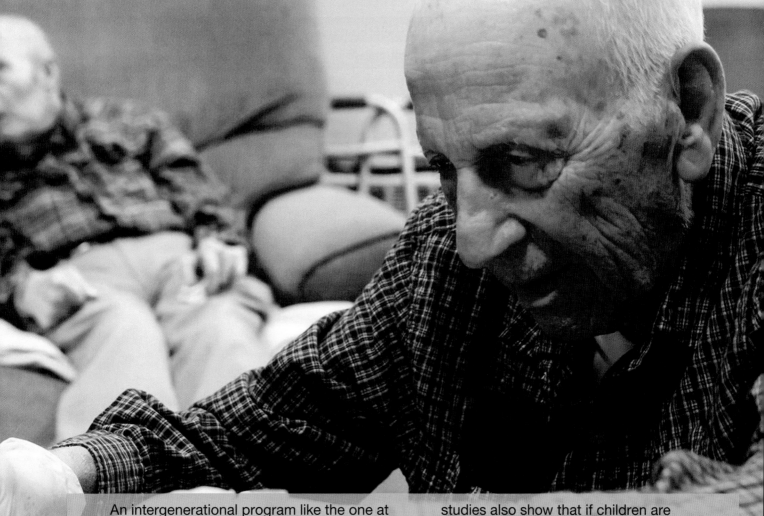

An intergenerational program mixes people of different ages... in this case, the very young and the very old!

An intergenerational program like the one at Providence Mount St. Vincent has clear
20 benefits. For the older people, their social life improves; they read to and play games with the children and encourage them in a wide range of other activities. Being involved with the children makes the seniors feel useful and
25 happy, and if they feel happy, their overall mental and physical health may improve.

The children also benefit from the program. They have an enthusiastic and patient group of people to play with in a safe environment.
30 Some of the seniors are also disabled,[2] and

studies also show that if children are exposed to people with disabilities at a young age, they will learn to be more tolerant and understanding of people
35 like this.

Providence Mount St. Vincent was even featured in a documentary film called *Present Perfect*. As families of both the young and the old see the benefits, intergenerational
40 programs are expanding. The film's message is starting to spread: even if the very young and the very old don't have a shared past or future, their shared present can be perfect.

[2]A *disabled* person has an illness or injury that makes doing certain physical or mental activities (like walking or thinking) difficult.

4 GRAMMAR

A Turn to pages 78–79. Complete the exercises. Then do **B–D** below.

Future Real Conditionals	
If clause	**Result clause**
If a woman **works**,	(then) a family **will have** more money.*
If we **don't protect** our open spaces,	(then) future generations **won't have** places to relax.
Result clause	**If clause**
A family **will have** more money	if a woman **works**.

*If you aren't certain, you can use *might (not)* or *may (not)* in a result clause:
*If a woman works, a family **may / might have** more money.*

B 🔄 Complete the sentences with a partner. How many sentences can you make? Make follow-up sentences for each one.

> If people have smaller families,…

> If you eat too many sweets,…

> If you eat too many sweets, you'll probably get sick.

> And if you get sick, you might miss class.

C Take out five small pieces of paper. On each piece, write an *if* clause like the examples in **B**.

D 🔺 Work in a small group. Follow the steps below.

1. Put all your papers together and mix them. Put them face down on the desk in a pile.

2. One person begins. Turn over a paper. You have 15 seconds to complete the sentence.
   - If you make a correct sentence, you get a point. Then put the paper aside.
   - If you don't make a correct sentence, put the paper at the bottom of the pile.

3. Then the next person goes. Play until you use all the papers. Who got the most points?

5 WRITING

A Read the paragraph. What is the writer predicting? Under the paragraph, circle your opinion.

> In the future, robots will do more of our jobs. Robots already work in some places today, like factories and restaurants. In five to ten years, you may see them in hospitals and schools. They'll even drive cars. Will this improve our lives?

In my opinion, it will / won't.

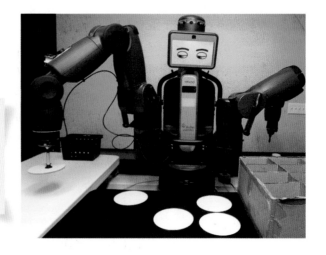

B Complete the outline below with ideas to support your answer choice in **A**.

If robots do more of our jobs, what will happen? Why is this good or bad?

_____

If the above happens, what will happen?

_____

If that happens, what will happen?

_____

For these reasons, I think robots doing more of our jobs will / won't improve our lives.

In your outline, think about how one event affects another: If A happens, then B might happen. If B happens, then C might happen.

C Write a paragraph with your opinion. Begin by writing the paragraph in **A**. Then continue your paragraph using your ideas from the outline in **B**.

D 🔁 Exchange your writing with a partner. Read his or her paragraph.

1. Are there any mistakes? If yes, circle them.

2. What is your partner's opinion and what reasons does he or she give? Do you agree?

3. Return the paper to your partner. Make corrections to your own paragraph.

6 COMMUNICATION

A Read each problem and suggest solutions for each one. Add your own ideas, too.

Problem: Too many young people are leaving rural areas and moving to big cities.

Suggestions:

1. _Give people money to encourage them to stay in their hometowns._

2. _Ask companies to provide_ _____

Problem: There's too much suburban development, and this is causing sprawl.

Suggestions:

1. _Limit the number of new homes being built each month._

2. _Support a law to_ _____

B Imagine you are running for political office. Prepare a short speech. Explain what you'll do to solve the problems in **A**.

C 👥 Work in a group of four people. Follow the steps below.

1. **Students A & B:** Give your speeches to the group.

   Students C & D: Listen and take notes. At the end, decide: Whose speech was better? Why?

2. Change roles and repeat step 1.

> Too many young people are leaving our area and moving to the city for jobs. If I get elected, I'll...

1 STORYBOARD

A Mr. Stevens and his son, Ian, are waiting in the doctor's office. Look at the pictures and complete the conversations. More than one answer is possible for each blank.

B 🔲 Practice the conversations in groups of four. Then change roles and practice again.

C 🔁 With a partner, create and perform your own conversation between a doctor and a patient.

2 SEE IT AND SAY IT

A 🔁 Look at the picture. Use the words in the box to talk about it. Then answer the questions with a partner.

campaign	election	speech
candidate	enthusiastic	term
citizens	running for (a political office)	

- Is this Mr. Gold's first political campaign?
- Look at the banner. Which of these ideas does Mr. Gold support?

  building more schools   encouraging public transportation

  raising taxes   stopping business development

- Who do you think will vote for Mike Gold? Who is going to vote against him?

B Work with a partner. Write a brief speech for Mike Gold. Perform your speech for another pair.

C Work with a partner. Write a brief speech for a candidate running against Mike Gold. Perform your speech for another pair.

3 I'M EXHAUSTED BECAUSE...

A 🔁 Match Camille's behaviors on the left with the causes on the right. Compare your answers with a partner's.

1. Camille is stressed out.

2. She's dizzy and hungry.

3. She's breathing hard.

4. She's shivering.

5. She's just swallowed two aspirin.

a. She's been playing tennis for two hours.

b. She forgot to bring her coat.

c. She works too much.

d. She skipped breakfast and lunch.

e. She has a headache.

B In two to three minutes, add as many items as you can to each category.

Things that make you...

1. cough: *cigarette smoke,* _____

2. feel exhausted: _____

3. feel dizzy: _____

4. shiver: _____

C 🔁 Ask a partner questions beginning with *What makes you...?* for each category in **B**.

4 TERRY'S DIARY

A Use the words in the box to complete Terry's diary entry about living in the city. (Three words are extra.)

action	opportunities
active	pollution
activity	taxes
affordable	traffic
dirty	transportation
in	with

Last night I went out with some old friends. They're all married and live in the suburbs. I'm single and still live in the city. They wanted to know why I still live here.

It's true—living in the city can be annoying sometimes. We have a problem with (1.) _____ streets. Plus, there's a lack of (2.) _____ housing. Everything is so expensive! The air (3.) _____ is pretty bad, too. You have to deal (4.) _____ a lot of these kinds of hassles every day.

On the other hand, the city is pretty great! First of all, there are a lot of job (5.) _____ here. I certainly have a well-paying job! The (6.) _____ can be pretty bad, but I avoid it. I take public (7.) _____ everywhere. I also stay (8.) _____ by walking all over the city.

The city is where all the (9.) _____ is, and I love it here!

B 🔁 What kind of hassles (difficult or frustrating situations) do you have to deal with in your city or town? Make a list with a partner.

5 POKER TIPS

A Read the advice given by a professional about how to play poker well. Rewrite each tip in reported speech, using the verb in parentheses.

1. Learn the different kinds of cards. (tell)

   _____

2. Don't bet too much money. (ask)

   _____

3. Study the other players' facial expressions. (ask)

   _____

4. Don't take unnecessary risks. (tell)

   _____

B Now think of a sport or game that you know how to play. Complete the sentences below. Don't show anyone!

People: There are... people on each team. / You play by yourself.

Equipment: The game is played with...

Location: It's played in / on...

Playing the game: The game starts when...

How to win: The object of the game is...

C 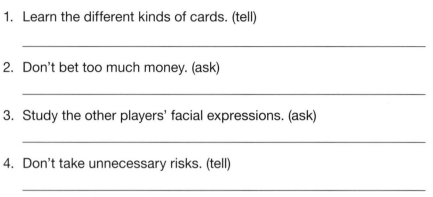 With a partner, take turns asking and answering questions about each other's sport or game. Can you guess what it is?

> Is it a sport?
>
> No. It's a card game.

> How many people play it?
>
> Four to six people play it. There aren't any teams—you play by yourself.

6 LISTENING

A 🔊 You are going to hear a lecture. Complete the notes. Write no more than two words for each answer. Then answer the question below.
Track 25

In which class would you probably hear this lecture?

☐ science
☐ math
☐ business

I. Dehydration: defined

A. Most of your body's weight is due to _____ —about _____%.

B. Dehydration occurs when the amount of water _____ the body is greater than the amount _____.

   1. "I'm dehydrated" means _____.

II. Causes

A. You can become dehydrated when you _____ a lot or are _____ on a hot day.

III. Symptoms

A. Include a _____ and getting _____.

   1. If you remain dehydrated, you may have to go to the _____.

7 STORYBOARD

A Lisa is asking Ana about her recent vacation. Look at the pictures and complete the conversation. More than one answer may be possible for each blank.

B Practice the conversation with a partner. Then change roles and repeat.

C What do you think of Ana's idea? What would you do to raise awareness? Tell a partner.

8 SEE IT AND SAY IT

A 🔁 Study the picture for ten seconds and then close your book. With a partner, take turns describing the scene in as much detail as you can.

B 🔁 Look at the picture again. Answer the questions with a partner.

1. Who are these people? Where are they?

2. Where are they going or what are they looking for? What time of day is it?

3. What do you think the leader is thinking?

C 🔁 What would you do if you were the leader of the group? Make suggestions and explain your answers with a partner.

> It's getting late. They should stop. If I were the leader, I'd suggest we sleep in the cave.

> That's one idea. But then again, I think the cave would be too cold. I'd suggest...

9 SARA AND SANDRA

A Read the story about Sara and Sandra. Fill in the missing words.

Sara and Sandra are sisters. They both _____ it rich by _____ the lottery.

Sara decided she could _____ by on very little money. She made a very tight budget for herself. She took 50 percent of the money and _____ it to charities. She also _____ aside the _____ amount in a bank _____.

Sandra, on the other hand, did something different. She _____ her money on jewelry, vacations, and presents for herself. She spent way _____ much money and didn't _____ anything. In one year, she had _____ into debt and _____ afford to pay _____ all the money she had borrowed.

B 🔁 With a partner, compare your answers in **A**.

C 🔁 Imagine your friend has won the lottery. Give him or her some financial advice. Use the negative modals in the box.

don't have to	had better not	shouldn't

> Well, for one thing, you don't have to tell everyone right away.

10 LISTENING

A 🔊 Listen to each response. Then choose the question that came before the response. **Track 26**

1. a. ☐ What does she look like?
   b. ☐ What's she like?

2. a. ☐ Why did you buy a new car?
   b. ☐ Why do you want a new car?

3. a. ☐ What would you do if you won the contest?
   b. ☐ What will you do when you win the contest?

4. a. ☐ Did you like the painting?
   b. ☐ How long did it take you to paint it?

5. a. ☐ When did they complete the bridge?
   b. ☐ When will they complete the bridge?

6. a. ☐ What do you usually do on Friday night?
   b. ☐ What do you want to do on Friday night?

11 WHILE YOU WERE OUT

A  Imagine that, while your boss was out, you took several messages. Work with a partner. Using reported speech, give the messages to your boss. Then switch roles and repeat.

> **Student A:** Give these messages to your boss.
>
> 1. Mary: "The meeting is scheduled for 2:00."
> 2. Tom: "I won't be in the office next week. I'll be in China on business."
> 3. Copy company: "We're running behind schedule on your job."
>
> **Student B:** Give these messages to your boss.
>
> 1. Celine: "I can't make the deadline."
> 2. Dry cleaners: "Your suits are ready."
> 3. Mario: "I don't understand your memo. I have questions about it."

> Were there any messages while I was out?

> Yes. There were three. Mary called. She said that...

12 MAKING PLANS

A With a partner, choose a situation and create a conversation of eight to ten sentences.

Situation 1	Situation 2
Student A: There's a Broadway show in town, and your partner wants to see it. You think the show is too expensive.	**Student A:** There's a popular art exhibit at the museum. Your partner wants to see it. You think it will be very crowded and hard to see the paintings.
Student B: There's a Broadway show in town, and you really want to see it. Persuade your partner to go.	**Student B:** There's an exhibition at the museum in town, and you really want to see it. Persuade your partner to go.

B: I really want to see the Broadway show that's in town.

A: Yes, but it's too expensive.

B: That's true, but...

B Practice your conversation. Then perform it for another pair.

LESSON A

Vocabulary

argue / argument
   get into an argument
converse / conversation
   strike up / start a
      conversation
   carry on a conversation
chat / chat
   chat with your coworkers
discuss / discussion
   a discussion of (the plan)
gossip / gossip
   the latest gossip
   a piece of gossip
   juicy gossip
share
   share your (feelings / ideas)
talk / talk
   give a talk, listen to a talk

argue / converse / chat / gossip /
   share / talk (*with* someone,
   about something)
discuss (something *with*
   someone)
have a(n) argument / conversation /
   chat / discussion / talk

Speaking Strategy

Interrupting someone politely
Introducing yourself
Excuse me. May I interrupt for
   a moment? My name is…
I'm sorry to interrupt. / I beg your
   pardon.
I just wanted to introduce myself.
   My name is…

Interrupting someone you know
Excuse me. Sorry to bother you,
   (name), but I have a question.
Could I interrupt for a second?
   I just wanted to say / ask
   something.

LESSON B

Vocabulary

media
in the media

news
get (your) news
in the news
tell (someone) the news
(news) **source**
news **story**
(**local / national / international**)
   news
(**entertainment / sports /**
   tabloid) news
(news) **program / site**
bad, good, great, sad,
   sensational (news)
spread the, hear the news

accurate ↔ inaccurate
reliable ↔ unreliable
scandal

word of mouth

UNIT 2 BUSINESS AND MARKETING

LESSON A

Vocabulary

advertise → advertisement → advertiser

consume → consumption → consumer

develop → development → developer

employ → employment → employer

invest → investment → investor

manage → management → manager

produce → production → producer

promote → promotion → promoter

purchase

ship → shipment → shipper

Speaking Strategy

Asking about companies
What does your company do exactly?
What is the main focus of your company?
How do you… ?

Emphasizing important points
I'd like to emphasize that…
Never forget that…
This is a key point.
The bottom line is…

LESSON B

Vocabulary

catchy

clever

a **dramatic increase / increase dramatically**

get better ↔ get worse

increase ↔ decrease

inspiring

persuasive

profits

recover

a **sharp fall / fall sharply**

shocking

a **slight rise / rise slightly**

(in a) **slump**

a **steady decline / decline steadily**

(be) up ↔ (be) down

UNIT 3 OUR WORLD

LESSON A

Vocabulary

dense

endangered

environment

extinct

habitat

illegal

increase ↔ **decline**

protected

raise awareness

rare / **rarely**

remain

suffer

(in the) **wild**

wilderness

Speaking Strategy

Offering another opinion
That's true, but…
Yes, but on the other hand,…
Even so,…
But then again,…

LESSON B

Vocabulary

accommodate

considered

construction

dam

dike

efficient

erode

force (someone to do something)

get around

goods

low-lying

obstacle

project

proposed

snapshot

sustainable

tear down (a building)

tenant

transport

withstand

LESSON A

Vocabulary

as usual
campaign
candidate
citizen
clear (adj)
corporation
enthusiastically
expand
give it your best shot
launch (v)
make progress
never in my wildest dreams
raise taxes
(a) record turnout
reelect
running neck and neck
tax (v)
term
up for reelection
vote (for ↔ against)
voting age
vow (v)

Speaking Strategy

Language for presentations

Stating the purpose
Today, I'd like to talk to you
  about…
I'll begin by (talking about the
  issue). / I'll provide an overview
  of (the issue).
Then I'll list the (two / three /
  four)…

Stating important points
Let's talk first about… / Let's start
  by talking about…
One of the main causes of (traffic)
  is…
Another / A second cause
  of (traffic) is…
And finally…

LESSON B

Vocabulary

a change of scene
depression
destroy → **destruction**
develop → **development**
disabled
encourage → **encouragement**
force → **force**
improve → **improvement**
protect → **protection**
provide
put down roots
rely (on) → **reliance**
sprawl
spread
suburban
support → **support**
urban
wait and see
waste → **waste**

UNIT 1 GETTING INFORMATION

LESSON A

Participial and Prepositional Phrases		
Who is Joe Ortega?	He's the guy	**chatting on the phone.** **on the phone.**
Who is Ms. Anh?	She's the woman	**wearing glasses.** **in front of the class.**
Which books are mine?	They're the ones	**lying on the floor.** **in the drawer.**

Use participial and prepositional phrases to identify people and things. These statements answer questions that ask *who*, *what*, and *which one(s)*.

A present participle uses the form verb + *-ing*. It follows the noun it is modifying: *She's the lady talking to the police officer*.

A prepositional phrase starts with *in*, *on*, *by*, etc. It also follows the noun it is modifying: *He's the man with the mustache*.

A Look at the picture below. What are the people doing? Give each person a name and write a sentence about him or her. Then label the picture.

Who is _____?

He's the man _____.

_____

_____

_____

_____

_____

_____

B Write questions about the people in the picture. (Use the words in parentheses.)
Start your questions with *Do you know...?*

1. (talk / bus driver) _____ Do you know the woman talking to the bus driver? _____

2. (listen / music) _____

3. (skateboard and backpack) _____

4. (school uniforms) _____

5. (talk / phone) _____

6. (suit / briefcase) _____

C 🔗 One a piece of paper, make up your own stories about each person. Use participial and prepositional phrases.

LESSON B

Review of the Present Perfect				
Subject	***have / has*** *(not)*	**Past participle**		
❶ I	**have**(n't)	seen	that news program.	
❶ He	**has**(n't)			
❷ I	**have**(n't)	worked	as a news reporter	**for** six months.
❷ She	**has**(n't)			**since** May.

❶ You can use the present perfect to talk about past actions or experiences when the time they happened is unknown or unimportant.
I have seen that news program.
I haven't been to France.

❷ Use can also use the present perfect to talk about an action that started in the past and continues up to now. Use *for* + a length of time. Use *since* + a point in time.
I have worked as a reporter for six months.
I've lived in Paris since May.

Notice the difference:
present perfect: I've worked as a news reporter for six months. I love my job. (action continues)
simple past: I worked as a news reporter for six months after college. (action is finished)

Questions and short answers					
Wh- word	**have / has**	**Subject**	**Past participle**		**Answers**
	Have	you	heard	the news?	**Yes, I have.** I heard it this morning.* No, I haven't. What happened?
How long	**have**	you	been	a reporter?	(I**'ve been** a reporter) **for** six months.
	has	she			(She**'s been** a reporter) **since** May.

* When you answer a present perfect question with a specific time expression, use <u>the simple past</u>:
Have you heard the news? Yes, I <u>heard</u> it <u>this morning</u>.

A 🎧 Complete the conversation. Use the present perfect form of the verb in parentheses, a short answer, or *for* or *since*.

A: (1. hear) ___Have___ you _____ the latest news about Leo?

B: No, I (2.) _____. What's up?

A: He's going to be on that reality show *Pop Idol*.

B: Really? How long (3. be) _____ Leo _____ a singer?

A: (4.) _____ high school.

B: I had no idea. (5. see) _____ you ever _____ him perform?

A: Yeah, I (6.) _____. I saw him at a talent show in high school. He was amazing.

UNIT **2** BUSINESS AND MARKETING

LESSON A

The Passive Voice: Simple Present and Simple Past			
Subject	**Verb**	**Object**	**Active voice**
Sound Smart	makes	audiobooks.	In an active sentence, the subject is the *agent* (the one performing the action).

Subject	**be**	**Past participle**	**(by + Object)**	**Passive voice**
❶ Audiobooks	**are**	**made**	by Sound Smart.	In a passive sentence, the object becomes the subject, and the subject becomes the object. The subject is not the agent because it doesn't perform an action.
❷ The products	**were**	**shipped**.		
❸ The company	**was**	**founded**	by Beverly Smith.	

❶ In a passive sentence, the focus is on the action that happens to the subject, not on who / what performed the action (the agent).

  Use *by* + object to indicate the agent: *The Fallingwater house **was built** <u>by Frank Lloyd Wright</u>.*

❷ We don't use *by* + object when the agent is understood, unknown, or unimportant, or when an action is done by people in general.

I'm paid twice a month. (I know who pays my salary. The agent is understood.)

*All of the money **was stolen**.* (We don't know who did it. The agent is unknown.)

*Once a week, her house **is cleaned**.* (We don't care who does it. The agent is unimportant.)

*Portuguese **is spoken** in Brazil.* (Everyone speaks it. It's done by people in general.)

❸ We include *by* + object in sentences where it sounds incomplete without it.
  The company was founded. (By whom? When? This sentence sounds incomplete.)
  We can also add a time or place phrase. *The company was founded (by Pablo Ruiz) (in Seattle) (in 2004).*

  The form of *be* depends on the verb tense. For the simple present, use *am / is / are* (see sentence ❶).
  For the simple past, use *was / were* (see sentences ❷ and ❸).

A Read this profile of Unilever, one of the world's largest companies. Find and circle six examples of the passive.

- Unilever was created in 1930 by a British soap maker and Dutch margarine producer.
- Today 400 brands of home, personal care, and food products are sold by the company.
- Some of the more popular products are Knorr® (soups), Lipton® (tea), and Dove® (soap).
- Lux® soap, which was introduced in 1924, became the first mass-marketed soap in the world.
- Today Knorr® is Unilever's most popular brand. It is sold in over 80 countries.
- The multinational company operates companies and factories on every continent except Antarctica.
- 174,000 people are employed by the company worldwide.
- 160 million times a day, a Unilever product is purchased by someone—somewhere in the world.

B Now rewrite the passive sentences in **A** as active sentences.

1. In 1930, _____ a British soap maker and Dutch margarine producer created Unilever. _____
2. Today the company _____.
3. In 1924, a man _____.
4. Today Unilever _____ in over 80 countries.
5. _____ 174,000 people.
6. 160 million times a day, someone in the world _____.

LESSON B

Connecting Ideas with *because, so, although / even though*	
❶ She uses that product **Because** it's the cheapest,	**because** it's the cheapest. she uses that product.
❷ This snack is "100% natural,"	**so** a lot of moms buy it for their kids.
❸ Many people buy that car **Even though / Although** it's expensive,	**even though / although** it's expensive. many people buy that car.

Because, so, although, and *even though* join two clauses together. A clause has a subject and a verb.

❶ *Because* answers the question *why*. It gives a reason: *Why does she buy that product? (She buys it) because it's the cheapest.*

In conversation, people often give the reason only (*because it's the cheapest*). Don't do this in formal writing. When the clause with *because* comes first, put a comma at the end of the clause.

❷ *So* gives a result: *The snack is "100% natural."* The result: *A lot of moms buy it.*

In writing, use a comma before *so* unless the two clauses are very short.

❸ *Although* and *Even though* mean the same thing, and they introduce <u>surprising or opposite information</u>: *Many people buy that car <u>even though it's expensive</u>.*

In writing, when the clause with *although / even though* comes first, put a comma at the end of the clause.

A Complete the sentences with *although / even though, because,* or *so*.

1. The phone was on sale, _____ *so* _____ many people bought it _____ they didn't need a new phone.

2. A lot of people buy those shoes _____ a famous basketball player wears them.

3. _____ their product is affordable, it doesn't work as well as ours.

4. The new toy was very popular, _____ it sold very quickly.

5. _____ smoking can kill you, many smoking ads show people smiling.

B Use the connecting words to join the sentences together. Which items can you write in more than one way?

1. That ad is really popular. It has a catchy slogan. (because)

   _____

2. I hate TV commercials. I don't watch much television. (so)

   _____

3. Advertising on TV is very expensive. Companies still do it. (although)

   _____

4. I still bought it. That TV is expensive. (even though)

   _____

5. I decided to try it. My sister liked that shampoo. (so)

   _____

LESSON A

Embedded Questions	
To *embed* means to put (something) inside something else. Embedded questions are questions that are included within another question or statement.	
What is a tapir?	Do you know **what a tapir is**?
	I'd like to know **what a tapir is**.
Although we call them embedded <u>questions</u>, they take <u>statement</u> word order.	
How many snow leopards are there?	I wonder **how many snow leopards there are**.
Where do mountain gorillas live?	Do you remember **where mountain gorillas live**?
What is the answer?	I'm not sure **what the answer is**.
These phrases are used to start embedded questions:	
Asking for information	**Saying you don't know something**
Can / Could you tell me…	I don't know / I'd like to know…
Do you know…	I'm not sure…
Do you remember…	I can't remember…
Do you have any idea…	I wonder…
An embedded question can sound softer and less direct than a regular question.	
Excuse me, what time is it?	Excuse me, do you know **what time it is**?

A Unscramble the embedded questions.

1. what / wonder / time / I / opens / it

   _____

2. are / zoo / animals / in / I / what / don't / the / know

   _____

3. I / remember / there / get / how / to / can't / exactly

   _____

4. any / animals / zoo / are / what / the / have / in / you / idea / do

   _____

5. time / it / sure / I'm / opens / what / not

   _____

6. to / do / zoo / you / get / know / to / the / how

   _____

B Now use the sentences in **A** to complete the conversation.

A: Excuse me, _____?

B: _____, but I think you take the #2 train.

A: _____.

B: _____, but it's probably open by now.

A: _____?

B: I'm sorry, but _____.

LESSON B

The Passive with Various Tenses		
	Active	**Passive**
Simple present	Engineers <u>build</u> skyscrapers with a steel frame structure.	Most skyscrapers **are built** with a steel frame structure.
Simple past	The Woolworth Company <u>built</u> a skyscraper in 1913.	One of the first skyscrapers **was built** in 1913.
Present perfect	Engineers <u>have built</u> the world's tallest building in Dubai.	The world's tallest building **has been built** in Dubai.
Present continuous	Engineers <u>are building</u> a lot of tall buildings in Shanghai.	A lot of tall buildings **are being built** in Shanghai.
Simple future	Someday they <u>will build</u> a skyscraper without concrete.	Someday a skyscraper without concrete **will be built**.

A Here are some facts about three important structures. Complete the sentences with the verb and tense in parentheses. Use the passive form of the tense provided.

Itaipu Dam

1. The dam (complete / simple past) _____ in 1991.

2. It (visit / present perfect) _____ by more than nine million people.

Akashi Kaikyo Bridge

3. The record for the longest suspension bridge (hold / simple present) _____ by the Akashi Kaikyo Bridge.

4. The bridge (design / simple past) _____ to be 12,825 feet, but it (make / simple past) _____ even longer after a big earthquake.

Chunnel

5. The first passengers on a Chunnel train were surprised when they (transport / simple past) _____ to the other side in only 20 minutes.

6. In the future, experts predict that even more passengers (carry / simple future) _____ through the Chunnel.

7. While repairs (do / present continuous) _____ to the tunnels, they remain open.

B Think of a famous building, structure, or monument in your city. Answer the questions about it using the passive.

1. Where is it located?

_____

2. When was it built?

_____

3. How many people have visited it?

_____

4. Are any repairs (fixes) being done to it now?

_____

5. What repairs will need to be done in the future?

_____

LESSON A

Too + Adjective / Adverb; *too much* / *too many* + Noun				
	too	**Adjective / Adverb**	**(Infinitive)**	
You're 17. You're	**too**	young	to vote.	
I can't understand him. He speaks	**too**	quickly.		
	too much* / *too many	**Noun**	**(Infinitive)**	
	Too much	pollution		is bad for your lungs.
Our city has	**too many**	problems	to solve	in one day.

Too means "to a greater degree than is acceptable." It often has a negative meaning.

It comes <u>before</u> adjectives and adverbs.

Use *too much* <u>before</u> noncount nouns.

Use *too many* <u>before</u> plural count nouns.

Adjective / Adverb + *enough*; *enough* + Noun				
	Adjective / Adverb	***enough***	**(Infinitive)**	
I'm 21. I'm	old	**enough**	to vote.	
These are good seats. I can hear	well	**enough.**		
	enough	**Noun**	**(Infinitive)**	
We have	**enough**	water	to get by	for now.
They have	**enough**	police officers		on the street.

Enough means "as much as you need" or "as much as is necessary."

It comes <u>after</u> adjectives and adverbs.

It comes <u>before</u> nouns (count and noncount).

A Complete the reasons on the right with *too*, *too much*, *too many*, or *enough*. Then match the questions with the answers.

1. Why are you so hungry now? _____
2. Why does your stomach hurt? _____
3. Why did you fail the driving test? _____
4. Why didn't you take the driving test? _____
5. Why did you lose the race? _____
6. Why are you running indoors? _____
7. Why did they close the bridge? _____
8. Why didn't you jump off the diving board? _____

a. Because I'm _____ young to drive.
b. Because I ate _____ candy.
c. Because there were _____ people on it.
d. Because it's _____ hot outside.
e. Because I didn't study hard _____.
f. Because I didn't eat _____ breakfast.
g. Because I wasn't brave _____.
h. Because I ran _____ slowly.

B 🔄 Correct the errors with *too* or *enough* below. Check your answers with a partner.

1. I can't button this shirt. It isn't too big.

2. It's not dangerous here. It's enough safe to go out at night by yourself.

3. It's crowded. There are too much people in this little room.

4. These condos are expensive enough to buy. We need more affordable housing.

5. He's only 12 years old. He's old enough to get a driver's license.

LESSON B

Future Real Conditionals	
If clause	**Result clause**
A: What will happen if a woman works? B: If a woman **works**,	(then) a family **will have** more money.
A: What will happen if we don't protect our open spaces? B: If we **don't protect** our open spaces,	(then) future generations **won't have** places to relax.
Result clause	**If clause**
A family **will have** more money	if a woman **works**.

Future real conditionals are used to talk about possibilities or to make predictions. The *if* clause states a possible situation. The result clause says what will or might happen.

The verb in the *if* clause uses <u>the simple present</u>. Don't say: *If a woman will work...*

The verb in the result clause uses <u>a future form</u>. You can also say, for example: *If we don't protect our open spaces, future generations **aren't going to have** places to relax.*

If you aren't certain about the result, you can use *might (not)* or *may (not)* in a result clause:
*If a woman works, a family **may / might have** more money.*

At the start of the result clause, you can use or omit the word *then*. Don't use *then* if the result clause comes first.

The result clause can come first in a sentence with no change in meaning.

In writing, when the *if* clause comes first, put a comma before the result clause.

A Use the simple present or future of the verbs in the box to complete the sentences.

be	~~get~~	make	not pass	not say	not study
educate	have	leave	miss	~~save~~	see

1. You _____'ll save_____ money if you _____get_____ a roommate.

2. If I _____ all weekend, I _____ the test on Monday.

3. I _____ hello if I _____ him on the street.

4. If you _____ early, you _____ all the fun.

5. It _____ better for the Earth if couples _____ smaller families.

6. If we _____ people, they _____ better decisions.

B Find and correct the mistake in each sentence.

1. If more people will carpool, there will be less traffic on the roads.

2. The school is going to cancel the picnic if it raining tomorrow.

3. If the team won't win tomorrow's game, then they'll be out of the World Cup.

4. You'll make more money in the future if you will go to college.

5. If we destroy the forests, then many animals die.

6. I might visit Italy this summer if I will have enough money.

C For each sentence in **B**, think of one more result and write a conditional sentence. The conditional should be one that follows the sentence in **B**.

1. _If there is less traffic on the roads, people will be happier._

2. _If the school cancels the picnic,_ _____

3. _____

4. _____

5. _____

6. _____

ADDITIONAL GRAMMAR NOTES

	The Present Perfect vs. the Present Perfect Continuous				
	have / has + (*not*)	*been*	verb + *-ing*		
I	**have**(n't)	**been**	**doing**	much in my spare time.	Use the <u>present perfect continuous</u> for an action that started in the past and continues in the present.
She	**has**(n't)	**been**	**participating**	in the school play.	

Incorrect: ~~I've been taking this test three times already.~~ Correct: **I've taken** this test three times already.	To talk about a repeated action in the past, use the <u>present perfect</u>, not the <u>present perfect continuous</u>.

I've been playing cricket <u>since I was a child</u>. <center>=</center>**I've played** cricket <u>since I was a child</u>.	When you use *for* or *since* to indicate a specific period of time in the past, you can use the <u>present perfect continuous</u> or the <u>present perfect</u>. They have the same meaning.
I've been reading a book on long-distance running. I'm enjoying it. (The action is ongoing.) <center>≠</center>**I've read** a book on long-distance running. It was excellent. (The action is completed.)	Some sentences don't indicate a specific time in the past. Use the <u>present perfect continuous</u> for an action that is still happening. Use the <u>present perfect</u> for a completed action. These two sentences have different meanings.
I've been going to the gym a lot <u>lately</u>. <u>Recently</u> **I've been working out** more.	To emphasize that an action has been happening in the recent past up to now, use words like *lately* and *recently* with the <u>present perfect continuous</u>.
Incorrect: ~~I've been owning that car for ten years.~~ Correct: **I've owned** that car for ten years.	As with other continuous tenses, don't use stative verbs (such as *hear*, *like*, and *own*) with the <u>present perfect continuous</u>. Use the <u>present perfect</u> instead.
Incorrect: ~~I've been taking this test three times already.~~ Correct: **I've taken** this test three times already.	To talk about a repeated action in the past, use the <u>present perfect</u>, not the <u>present perfect continuous</u>.

A Tom has started a lot of activities but hasn't finished them. Write five affirmative sentences in the present perfect continuous using the verbs in the box. What is one activity that he hasn't started yet? Write one negative sentence. (Note: The verb *do* is used twice.)

do	eat	study	talk	watch

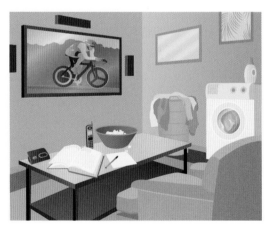

1. *He's been doing his homework.* _____
2. _____
3. _____
4. _____
5. _____
6. _____

B Circle the correct answer(s) to complete each sentence.

1. I've gotten / I've been getting increasingly active since I joined the judo club.
2. I've belonged / I've been belonging to the club for three months.
3. This is the third time I've taken part / I've been taking part in an extracurricular activity.
4. We've practiced / We've been practicing after school every day since April.
5. My sister has joined / has been joining the photography club.
6. She's taken / She's been taking pictures every day.

Review: The Simple Past vs. the Present Perfect vs. the Present Perfect Continuous		
	Completed past action	**Actions started in the past continuing up to now**
Simple past	❶ I **visited** South Africa <u>in 2010</u>.	
Present perfect	❷ I've **visited** South Africa once.	❸ Fabiola **has skated** for years.
Present perfect continuous		❹ Fabiola **has been skating** for years.

❶ Use the <u>simple past</u> to talk about completed (finished) actions.

❷ You can use the <u>present perfect</u> to talk about past actions if the time they happened is not stated.

In sentence ❶, the speaker says when he was in South Africa: <u>in 2010</u>. For this reason, the simple past is used.

In sentence ❷, the speaker has been to South Africa in the past, but he doesn't say when. The present perfect is used.

❸&❹ You can use the <u>present perfect</u> or the <u>present perfect continuous</u> with *for* or *since* to talk about an action that started in the past and continues up to now. Notice that sentences ❸ and ❹ have the same meaning.

Do NOT use the <u>present perfect continuous</u> in the situations below. Use the <u>present perfect</u> instead.

With stative verbs (verbs not used in the continuous like *be, have, like, hate, know, need*):

~~I've been knowing her for five years.~~   I've **known** her for five years.

To talk about actions that happened a specific number of times:

~~She has been winning the gold medal in the event six times.~~   She **has won** the gold medal in the event six times.

A Read about mountain climber Erik Weihenmayer. Complete the sentences with the verbs in parentheses. Use the present perfect or the present perfect continuous.

Erik Weihenmayer (1. be) _____ blind* since he was 13. He (2. climb) _____ since he was 16, and he's still doing it.

Erik (3. climb) _____ Mount Everest. Also, he (4. reach) _____ the top of the Seven Summits—the seven tallest mountains on the seven continents.

Erik (5. develop) _____ his own climbing system. His partners wear bells on their vests. He follows the sounds of the bells.

Erik (6. think) _____ about his next trip for a long time, but he (7. not choose) _____ a place to go yet.

blind = unable to see

B Circle the correct verb form to complete each sentence. Sometimes, both answers are possible.

I learned / I've learned how to play dominoes from my grandfather many years ago. He taught / He's been teaching me the game during my summer break from school.

My cousin is 20 years old. He played / He's been playing dominoes since he was seven years old. He's been / He's been being in many dominoes competitions. Last year he got / he's gotten second

(continued)

place in a really big contest. He's always done / He's always been doing well under pressure. I think he'll win first prize this year.

My grandfather has played / has been playing the game for 50 years. He says he's played / he's been playing about 20,000 games, and he doesn't plan to stop.

Answers

Communication page 37, A

1. Singapore **2.** Greenland **3.** Angel Falls **4.** Etna **5.** the Andes **6.** Mammoth Cave **7.** Lake Baikal **8.** the Sahara **9.** Canada

NOTES

NOTES

NOTES

NOTES

NOTES

NOTES

NOTES

NOTES

NOTES

NOTES

NOTES